APR 1 5 1999

The Harker School Library

DISCARD

W9-CSM-591

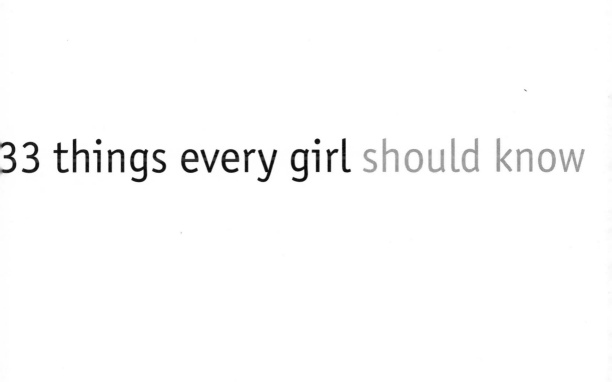

33 things every girl should know

33 things every girl should know

STORIES, SONGS, POEMS, AND SMART TALK
BY 33 EXTRAORDINARY WOMEN
edited by TONYA BOLDEN

The Harker School Library
500 Saratoga Avenue
San Jose, CA 95129

DISCARDED

CROWN PUBLISHERS, INC.
NEW YORK

Copyright © 1998 by Tonya Bolden
Front cover photograph copyright ©1997 by Jim Cummins / FPG International

All rights reserved. No part of this book may be reproduced or transmitted in any form or by any means, electronic or mechanical, including photocopying, recording, or by any information storage and retrieval system, without permission in writing from the publisher.

Photographic acknowledgments: The Body Shop, UK: pages 16, 17, 18. Tanya Burnett, copyright © 1997, courtesy of Lauren Hutton: page 54. Elizabeth Jenkins-Sahlin: page 102. The Office of the Architect of the Capitol: page 105. Dana Lixenberg, copyright © 1995: page 143. Gretchen Rosenkranz: pages 22, 24, 25, 27. Vera Wang Ltd.: pages 39, 40, 41, 42.

Acknowledgments for permission to reprint previously published material can be found on pages 158–159.

Published by Crown Publishers, Inc., a Random House company, 201 East 50th Street, New York, New York 10022.

CROWN is a trademark of Crown Publishers, Inc.

Book design by Elizabeth Van Itallie

http://www.randomhouse.com/

Printed in the United States of America

Library of Congress Cataloging-in-Publication Data

Bolden, Tonya.

33 things every girl should know / edited by Tonya Bolden.

    p.   cm.

Summary: A mix of short stories, essays, a comic strip, a speech, an interview, poems, and more which offer insights and advice for girls.

ISBN 0-517-70936-8 (trade pbk.) — ISBN 0-517-70999-6 (lib. bdg.)

1. Girls—Literary collections. [1. Girls—Literary collections. 2. Conduct of life—Literary collections.] I. Bolden, Tonya.

PZ5.A125   1998

810.8'092827—dc21   97-29431

10 9 8 7 6 5 4 3 2 1

First Edition

I am immensely grateful to Jill Davis for all she did in getting this book off the ground, as I am to my final editor, Andrea Cascardi, for the marvelous mind she devoted to the finish. I thank, too, those of the Crown crew who gave all sorts of support and assistance along the way: Simon Boughton, Nancy Hinkel (*real* trooper is she!), Nancy Siscoe, and Rebecca Stevens.

Many others have done much for this book: Christina Ambrosino, Luca Babini, Jennifer Baumgardner, Susan Bergholz, Pari Berk, Linda Brandon, Bobby Brunson, Jr., Julie Cooper, Kenton S. Edelin, Terry Gumz, Anastasia Higginbotham, Laurie Jakobsen, Coline Jenkins-Sahlin, Charles Johnson, Leslie Jones, Mary Mihalakos, Bonniee Mookherjee, Alison Oscar, Tara Poole, Mary Robbins, Tory Robinson, Paula Rosenkranz, Caroline Smith, Marsinay Smith, Eleanor Southworth, Arlene Stolz, Debbie Taylor, Georgia Tedla, Nan Thomas, Susy Westfall, and Carol Wood. All y'all's "little things" have meant a whole lot.

Special thanks to the wonderful womenfolk who know all about it and are always there for me: my sister Nelta Brunson; my sister in Christ, Elza Dinwiddie-Boyd; my agent, Marie Dutton Brown.

Last thing: Huge gratitude to the contributors for your generosity and grace.

co n t

e n t s

It's no secret. This book is about girl build-up.

ground Z

You're eleven, or twelve . . . or older. You've got questions—and confusions. At times your soul's song is a bracing melody, and then come moments when it is a blues tune with no name.

Maybe you are shy. Or perhaps you're prone to roar. Maybe all in your life is calm and dandy, or could be you are in chaos and too much has gone wrong.

Whatever the case, whatever your pace, this book has a great deal to offer. And it's a mix—short stories, essays, a comic strip, two comix, a letter, a speech, an interview, a "public-service announcement," poems, and more—from people who have walked in your shoes, and a few who are, agewise, right close to where you are now. They are all females of positive distinction: writers, entrepreneurs, visual artists, performing artists, educators, athletes. Most important, they are folks who cheer you, who wish you the best, who urge you to grow up steady and strong as you go about your girlhood and head on to womanhood.

Some share memories—of bewilderments, of wonderments, of sorrows, of fears. Others offer fresh takes on old truths. And then there are those who have zeroed in on a thing they wish somebody had talked with them about when they were eleven, or twelve . . . or older.

Wisdom. That's the ticket. It may not sound so hip, but trust me, it is absolutely what you need to be whole, stand tall, keep real. And while the thirty-three "things" you are about to encounter are not the only things you will ever need to know, they do represent a sound, solid start.

Me? I must admit I envy you a bit. I wish I'd had such a collection of girltalk as this when I was a teenager: a place I could go to again and again, all by myself, for advice, for private dreaming, for talking to my tears; a place, too, to find the kick to keep stepping—with an occasional leap!

Yeah, I found my way. But to have had as a part of my survival kit a book like this when I was eleven, or twelve . . . or older sure would have helped my journey.

—TONYA BOLDEN

(seize the day)

CARPE DIEM

by Judith Ortiz Cofer

Remember to wake early and take your time in rising.
Enter the world refreshed by the hope
emitted by each atom of light,
by the bird who must sing at the sight
of the sun. Does he pity us humans,
who can choose not to break into song
at dawn?

Look for small revelations all day.

Let water heal your body. Think of bathing
as a ritual of new beginnings.

Step outside and breathe deeply.
Take in the smells
of life, good and foul. Remember
this day is a gift.

Be surprised by nature
that shares your world of giant steps.
The bug that irks you, the yellow butterfly
that catches your eye,
and the furred thing with sharp teeth
that repels you—are all in your moment
of history.

Concentrate on living hour by hour as if
you were feeding coins into a meter
measuring your life.
Here is this hour,
and you have already paid for it.

Love your work, and enjoy your play. Remember,
there is little lasting joy in things done
only for gold or fame. Without love
your spirit will be a flower
picked without purpose
and thrown on the ground
to be trampled by anyone.

Have a place and a time
to sit with your thoughts.
Pray before sleep, or read a great poem.
Sacred words will clear your crowded mind.
Remind yourself to speak in Spanish
before you go into the dark.
Greet your ancestors
in our native tongue, let them guide you
to the place of your origin, an island in the sun,
our home now only in our dreams. Say *noche,*
say *amor,* say *sueños.*

Welcome the night. Good sleep
is your body's mending time. In its sweet release,
the fires of worry and anger will be subdued;
and in dreams you may learn to fly above any blaze,
and let your secret self float free
above a new world
you must imagine and learn to embrace
each and every day.

THE CROOKED PATH

has its dividends

by Sigourney Weaver

"I was not the brightest star in my class by far. I was always in a bit of trouble, nothing interesting. But my presence here today is a testament to all late bloomers."

This is from the opening of the commencement address I delivered in June 1990 at The Chapin School, an all-girls school in New York City which I attended. Several months before I spoke to them I visited with the senior class to better prepare for my "role," to better speak to their needs, their fears, their hopes.

The best part of any graduation comes when you're racing out the door. As you leave, you should know how esteemed you are as a class by the teachers and other students here. You have brought a generosity of spirit to this year's school days that will leave a kind and happy echo in the hallways. Now there will be no more regulations . . . no more uniforms. Now, the really interesting part of life begins: when the rules and conditions are of your own choosing. You have had years of solid education here; you have made precious friendships that will last all your lives; you have had the advantage of going to a single-sex school where you've been used to leading, to taking charge and getting things done—and we need women leaders today. You're ready. You're formed. You have this place down. It's time to go.

The first thing I would urge on each of you is to have faith in your inner compass. It will never let you down, although sometimes it will confound you. (To compass: "Why are you taking me this way when I want to go over there?" Or, "I want to go in the direction she's going. That looks really good.") Each of us has her own crooked path complete with detours, wrong turns, and dead ends. Even more frustrating, we have our own timetables! I wanted to get married at twenty-three and have a child at twenty-five. (I didn't really, but it sounded well organized.) As it turned out, I got married at thirty-four and had a child at forty. If you'd told me that when I was twenty, I would have been horrified. But I have to say, it's pretty perfect the way it's worked out.

Now I'm sure some of you today are going off to the perfect college and have the perfect boyfriend and the perfect summer job. Congratulations!— we hate you. But for those of you who do not, take heart. Things have a way of working out for the best—often in very surprising ways! When I graduated from high school, I was not going to my first choice of college or even my second choice. I was going to my lowly third choice—and when I got there I hated it. Despair . . . inertia. But then, after a year, I ended up transferring to a university out West, where I had never even thought of applying originally. And I loved it. The crooked path has its dividends.

Another thing you need besides your inner compass are your fearless shoes. I am wearing my fearless shoes today because I am not very comfortable as a public speaker. But self-doubt is not a good reason to say no to any new opportunity. We are all capable of so much more than we think.

Another bit of advice I can offer is: Don't depend on other people's encouragement. It's never enough and never when you need it. When I was at the Yale Drama School, I was told by the head of the acting department that I had no talent and should think about a different profession. I looked around the room at the other professors, some of whom knew better, and they looked away. If they disagreed with their boss, they didn't have the guts to say so. I was crushed. For a long time. You know how we all have this little voice that says "Hah! I knew you couldn't do it"? . . . Well, this little voice, which we all have—in stereo—made me feel sad and helpless for a long time. When I got out of school, though, everyone hired me, even some of those teachers. It still hurts, but now I make sure I always have my good puppet with me who says things like "That was great! What a good idea! You can do it!"

Excellence takes hard work and commitment. It's so easy to think it's a snap for everyone else. One automatically supposes that everybody else has it together. They may give that impression, but it's simply not true. Everyone has to struggle. Sometimes your biggest battle is to believe in yourself. Every time I get a new job I am overcome with anxiety. Perhaps it's a way of revving up the engine. When I went off to Africa to play Dian Fossey in *Gorillas in the Mist,* I was terrified: Would the gorillas eat me for breakfast? Would I be able to convey the complexity of Dian's character? How would I survive without cable for four months? When I got over there, I was too busy to think about these things. I just gave it my all.

As I neared the end of the speech, I told the audience about "one of those terrible questions" I'd been asked with regard to my daughter, Charlotte, who was then just a little over two months old.

What kind of world was I bringing her into? A world that boasts of Tiananmen Square, of the tragedies of Yusuf Hawkins and the Central Park jogger, of AIDS, drugs, poverty, indifference. Would there even be a world when she was old enough to have children? Part of my optimism about the future comes from meeting all of you. Your appraisal of the problems we face today, your refusal to be intimidated by them, and your vision of how to improve education, health, and communication among us in this country all inspire me. You're not going to mess around. I look forward to seeing what your ferocious young energies and commitment can teach the rest of us.

As you set off, I leave you with this poem:

"Come to the edge," I said.

"No, we're afraid."

"Come to the edge."

"No . . . We're afraid. We'll fall."

"Come to the edge," I said again.

And they came.

And I pushed them.

And they flew.

3

move!

by Anita Roddick

I am something of a nomad. I travel about five months a year, visiting as many of The Body Shop stores as possible in close to fifty countries and looking at small grassroots initiatives here and there, too. Travel, for me, isn't just about business: There's the splendor it holds as a university without walls.

My own life's journey began in Littlehampton, a small town on the south coast of England. A once very popular resort town, Littlehampton had lost its shimmer by the time I came along in the 1940s. Even still, there was lots of dazzle for me because of the Clifton Café, a family business my mother owned and ran.

The café, which was open from five o'clock in the morning until there were no more customers, dominated our lives. There were no family holidays. There were no family diversions except for a weekly trip to the cinema. After school and on weekends, as we got old enough for the tasks, my two sisters, my brother, and I were on duty, doing everything from taking orders and clearing tables to working behind the cash register. The Clifton Café was an extension of our home. And it was

16

wonderful: Courtships flourished there, friendships were born, the eye was delighted. Our café was a whole world of adventures and lessons.

My mother, through stories, took us on fantastic journeys. Not for us children's rhymes and riddles, but real stories—stories of romantic love, stories about how we were conceived, and stories about the world my mother knew growing up on a farm in southern Italy.

My mother also introduced us to the territory of deep, independent thinking. She reminds me of the wonderful Walt Whitman quote from the preface to the first edition of *Leaves of Grass*.

This is what you shall do: love the earth and sun and the animals, despise riches, give alms to everyone that asks, stand up for the stupid and crazy, devote your income and labor to others, hate tyrants, argue not concerning God, have patience and indulgence toward the people, take off your hat to nothing known or unknown

or to any man or number of men . . . re-examine all you have been told at school or church or in any book, dismiss what insults your own soul and your very flesh shall be a great poem.

And my mother pushed me to the edge of bravery. She challenged everything, and she created a world that allowed my spirit to flourish. Whenever I did anything kind or loving to anyone, she would delight in it.

Had it not been for my mother, I might never have become so enthralled with the woman I regard as my first historical heroine: Joan of Arc, who nearly six hundred years ago, at age seventeen, took up arms in defense of France's rightful king. Joan of Arc gave me moral imagination. She fought for what was right; she fought the god of conformism and apathy— always, always examining herself.

Many, many years before I became an entrepreneur, I was a teacher, and I carried the spirit of Joan of Arc with me into this endeavor. My task, I was certain, was to develop in my students purpose, imagination, a sense of truth, and a feeling of empathy and responsibility. I tried to move away from useless structures and curricula that produce mediocrity. For instance, when we were studying the works of World War I poets such as Rupert Brooke, I felt it would be much more meaningful to the students if we hitched to the Somme area in France and read the poems in the trenches, where the soldiers about whom Brooke wrote fought. Unfortunately, the idea wasn't received quite so well by the other teachers. Likewise, the teachers thought my methods a little off the wall when I painted the classroom walls with bright primary colors to spark the imagination, or when I played loud music, such as Gregorian chants, to transform the atmosphere of the classroom when we were studying the Reformation. Anything to set the minds of my students traveling.

In 1962, when I was nineteen, I went to Israel and worked on a kib-butz—where my day began at three o'clock in the morning! It was exhaust-ing but ultimately most exhilarating: I learned so much about Israel, about the cultures of its people, and about myself (like how invigorating hard work is for me). And I hitchhiked around this nation, mostly alone, but sometimes traveling a trail with other young men and women my age from other countries. In the 1960s, I never thought twice about hitchhiking any-where. Youth is fearless. But today I drive past hitchers and brood on how, with time, I've learned to be afraid.

This was my first major travel experience, however, and I knew I wanted to make travel a perpetual part of my life.

Many years since, The Body Shop has compelled much travel, and I have always held the belief that what gives me, and ultimately my company, an edge is that I get out of the chair, out from behind the desk, out of the office. And I *move*. I move toward people who have a vision clearer than mine, and toward those situations that allow me an education in real-life experiences.

There was the time I spent in what many regard as the most disadvan-taged Native American reservation: Rosebud in South Dakota, home to the Oglala Lakota Oyate. I had been invited by the tribal colleges to see if I could come up with a creative solution to any one of their huge social problems. Almost immediately I noticed that in the Badlands sage bush grew wild—and an idea was born: Gather the sage bush, extract the essen-tial oil, and convert it into personal-care products. Easy.

No. Not easy. First, they said, we had to ask permission from the plant nation. And we had to do a sweat. Then . . . maybe.

The sweat was a ritual whereby we entered a wigwam and sat around some hot embers. Sage bush was put onto the embers, and we sat in this circle and talked and prayed. As the embers died down, water was put on them so that the steam transformed the tent into a sweat lodge. We stayed there praying and talking until the embers died and we were left in total darkness. The experience led me to a deeper understanding that I am not superior to nature but rather a part of nature. It taught me something more than respect. It taught me reverence.

In 1994, I decided to take a journey through Alabama, Mississippi, and Louisiana. I felt I was in need of an antidote to the life I am comfortably living. Traveling through this region was my first experience with *real* poverty in a Western country. To be poor is hard, but to be poor in the United States, in a land of such wealth, is the very bottom of such hardship—like that known by a woman named Wilma, who was living in a one-room shack in the middle of a field near Montgomery, Alabama. She wouldn't come out of her house because her mother had just died, and to make matters worse, somebody had tortured her dog to death. I spent hours talking with her through the cracks in the walls. This woman, like so many of her neighbors, was living a purposeful life, going on hour by hour, minute by minute, engaged in a desperate struggle to survive and to be sheltered, living in a sort of maze that many never experience or even know about.

Contact with people living such hugely uncomfortable lives sharpened my insight into what a catastrophe poverty is. It also made me an even more dogged believer in small-scale projects that keep a community together and a culture intact while it builds it up economically. Viewed in isolation, these grassroots initiatives seem modest. Ten women planting a tree on a roadside . . . a dozen youths digging a well . . . an old man teaching neighborhood kids to read. Such things may not seem like a big deal to some, but they can add up to something monumental.

No one person can go everywhere. No one person can witness firsthand all the ways of living in the world. But we can always listen and learn from others. I have experienced many journeys "secondhand" that have transformed me, particularly from The Body Shop workers.

The people I work with are mostly young, mostly female. All are in search of present-day heroes and heroines. For them their work is about a search for daily meaning as well as for their daily bread, for recognition as well as cash, for astonishment rather than boredom. These people define power as the power in dreams, in curiosity, in music, in a reach for the human spirit. Their secret ingredient is enthusiasm. Enthusiasm created from the heart guides your whole system, so there is no resistance, and everything flows and seems possible. When a member of our staff, after spending three exhaustive weeks in a Romanian orphanage refurbishing the buildings or holding babies with AIDS, looks you dead in the eye and says, "This is the real me," you take heed, for she is dreaming of noble purposes, not a moisture cream.

The most insightful things I have learned firsthand from my travels are two simple truths about women. The first is this: It is still women who carry the double burden. Women in most societies—in the West, in the East, in developed and underdeveloped nations alike—carry the responsibility of caring for the family, from managing the household to being the one who drops everything when a child is ill. The second simple truth is that in practically all societies, women are victims of either discrimination or disadvantage, based most often on wealth, skin color, and education. Some women do suffer more discrimination than others, but this should not divide women. The common denominator of discrimination should unite us to create a real ragtag front line that pushes back environmental destruction and promotes women's rights and an alternative worldview to the one I encounter everywhere I travel: the worldview that favors the educated white male.

What and who you encounter as you go about your life is as important as whatever satisfies your immediate needs—your education, your future work, your family, your friends. You are the sum total of your experiences. The places, events, and people you experience make their mark on you like the curves and dots of some inward map that guides you through life.

So I say to you, *Move!* Now. There's no need to wait until you're a full-fledged adult to start enhancing the geography of your mind and spirit. Pick your parents' literature off the shelves to read; engage your grandparents in storytelling; question teachers, neighbors, community group leaders, and friends; wander around art galleries and libraries. Look for inspiration in every unexpected place—then share the information and stories you discover with a friend.

imagi

by Gretchen Rosenkranz

Imagine that . . . when you were six you got to meet the President of the United States . . . when you were seven you traveled to Scotland—clear across the world . . . when you were eight you got to be the queen for the mini-hydro races (racing remote-control hydroplanes) . . . when you were nine you got to ski down the magnificent mountains at Snoqualmie Pass in Washington State's Cascade Mountains . . . when you were ten you were setting national records in track . . . when you were eleven you were making a short movie with a professional director.

Imagine all these things happening to someone who did not take her first steps until she was four years old, a girl like me who cannot walk by herself but who must use crutches or leg braces or a wheelchair to get around.

I was born with spina bifida: with an open spine. On day one of my life, September 23, 1980, the doctors thought I would never walk.

When I was four years old, Mom started taking me to swimming lessons. At first I was terribly afraid of the water. I was afraid because I spent the first few years of my life in casts, so I didn't get a chance to learn not to be afraid as early as most kids. Thank goodness Mom believed that I could overcome the fear. And then my swimming instructor believed in me—and I learned to swim. By the time I was ten, I was able to join a swim team at Tumwater Valley, not far from my home. All the others on the team were regular kids, but the coach and kids accepted me just the same.

I can't kick, but I can swim, so the coach encouraged me to do the

n e . . .

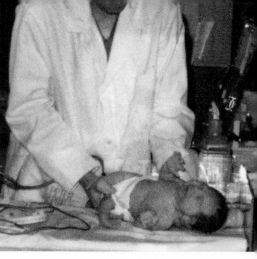

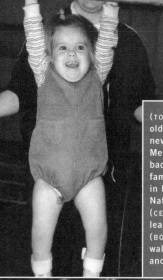

backstroke and freestyle. After a while I wanted to do the butterfly and the breaststroke, but the coach said I should just stick to the backstroke and freestyle. I did not want to give up my dream of learning the other two strokes, because I knew I had to do them to earn a medal in the individual medley.

(TOP RIGHT) One day old. They thought I'd never walk. (TOP LEFT) Me at 12 months, backpacking with my family at Ohanapecosh in Mount Rainier National Park. (CENTER) At 2½, Mom learns to let go. (BOTTOM) My first walker—I'm finally up and going.

A few months later I went to a sports day for kids like me at a local university. A woman in the pool was watching me swim. She couldn't believe what I could do without using my legs. I shared with her my goal of going to a national championship for young athletes in wheelchairs and swimming the breaststroke and the butterfly. She taught me those strokes that day. When I showed my coach what I had learned to do, she began helping me improve my technique. I practiced for the next two months. Then I had a minor setback: I broke my leg. I was in a cast for two months and resumed my swimming with only four months until the competition.

At the 1992 Junior National Wheelchair Championship Games in Orlando, Florida, I won bronze medals in the butterfly, the backstroke, and the individual medley. I made it happen. Yes, I had help, but only after I first believed.

With your imagination you can fly like an eagle. With your imagination you can dream on a

cloud. With your imagination anything you want to do can be done, and you can begin to make many things happen. Because I allowed myself to dream, my life has not been the tragedy some thought it would be.

Believing is the second key. When you are very young, your believing comes from mirroring those who believe in you. It might be parents, or grandparents, or other relatives. Maybe it is someone in a church or the next-door neighbor who takes a bit of time to listen and encourage an idea or a thought. Or is it a teacher with the patience and zest to inspire creative thinking? As you grow older, you must learn to believe in yourself even when others are questioning the possibilities you seek.

(TOP) I loved my hand cycle. I got it when I was 4. (CENTER) Me at age 9 with Casie Largent, 8, and her brother Krammer, 4, who also has spina bifida. (BOTTOM) Doing pushups with classmates in P.E.

When I was in preschool my dad ran a lot. I thought, Wouldn't it be fun if I could run with my dad someday? I told my mother about this one day, and she called around and found out about a sports conference at the University of Washington. A few years later, when I was old enough, I went to this neat sports day up there and tried a whole bunch of fun things. My favorite thing was wheelchair racing. Up there we met Jim Martinson, who made racing wheelchairs, and we set up an appointment to get me started. A few weeks later we called a group of adults who race and went out to meet them. I became a part of their team, the Olympia Rain Rollers. I started out racing in my standard wheelchair, and a few months

later I got a racing chair. My trainer, Bev, could hardly keep up. I entered my first race in 1990. It was two miles around the town of Tumwater, Washington.

A year later I raced in my first Junior National Wheelchair Championship Games in Princeton, New Jersey. I was the only girl on my team that year. I helped set a national record for a mixed 4 x 100 track relay.

That was the beginning of racing. I have had continued success with junior nationals in Florida, Ohio, Oklahoma, and Colorado. I have done every race from a 100 on the track to a half marathon on a hilly course in my hometown of Olympia, Washington. I hope to continue and do a full marathon.

Me at age 14 at
Capital Lake in
Olympia, Washington.

the winner is always the one with the
FEWEST
DOUBTS

by Nicole Haislett

There is a saying that "talent can only take you so far." I don't know who first said it, but I bet it came from a person who discovered this truth through experience.

During my eighteen years of swimming competitively, I often stood atop awards podiums receiving first-place honors, wondering how and why I had bested those who stood below me. When I finally came up with the answer, I knew it would be the same every time I asked myself. Simply stated, I had worked harder.

But how do you differentiate between just going through the motions (even if you do break a sweat) and getting your body near its breaking point? It wasn't until the end of my career that I was able to get a handle on the essence of hard work—and came up with my own definition: identifying your personal limits, and then pushing past them, and then setting new barriers, and then . . . repeating the process again and again. Most people don't try to explore, let alone reach their potential. Those who do become champions.

Throughout my years of swimming I always believed I was working "as hard as I could." But this changed in 1992 when I found myself on the United States Olympic Swim Team, and my great hope of winning a gold medal was so close. I bore down and trained harder than ever. As a result, I recorded times in practice and completed workouts I had once considered impossible. I would swim twice a day, lift weights, do the StairMaster, throw medicine balls, and use stretch cords to work on upper-body strength—all in one day. One afternoon my coach asked me to do six 75-yard swims. Each one that was faster than 37.5 seconds would count as two. So I swam the first three all faster than 37.0 seconds and was able to stop there. Every swim set I did was faster than anything I had done prior to it. I surprised myself by doing something better each day. It was almost as if I didn't feel any pain or fatigue.

Knowing how hard I had worked enabled me to stand behind the starting block with confidence, believing myself completely capable of winning. And I did: three gold medals.

In a way, it wasn't really the medals that filled me with so much pride. You see, the "thrill of victory" comes from knowing you have done everything possible to achieve your goal. There will never be a successful person who, before performing a task, has doubts. Negative thoughts arise from recognizing that somewhere along the line your level of commitment has dropped below 100 percent. The winner will always be the person with the fewest doubts.

All of this seems very easy—work hard, build your confidence, and victories will follow. The tricky part comes in when you realize that there are people all over the world who do these things. Many of them are very good at what they do, be it their singing, their painting, their sport. But what separates the good from the best? What is the difference between the person who makes it to the Olympics and the person who wins an Olympic gold medal, or the person who becomes a doctor and the doctor who wins a Nobel Prize for medicine?

From what I have seen, it is not ability, and it's not knowledge. It is the inner drive, the willpower, the focus—something no one can give you.

Those who truly have the spirit of champions are never wholly happy with an easy win. Half the satisfaction stems from knowing that it was the time and the effort you invested that led to your high achievement—not your good luck, not someone else's bad luck (and certainly not cheating).

And yes, as another unknown someone has said, "Winning isn't everything." If you don't turn out to be the straight-A student, or the lead ballerina, or the fastest swimmer, this does not mean you are a failure. Ultimately, success is not measured by first-place prizes. It's measured by the road you have traveled: how you have dealt with the challenges and the stumbling blocks you've encountered along the way.

Athletics is an area in which many people compete, and it is an incredible feeling to win, but most of life's challenges come outside the sports arena. Winning can be anything from passing a test to kicking a drug habit to walking again after a crippling accident. If you participate in sports, let the lessons you learn there carry over into the rest of your life. If you aren't into sports, borrow from the athlete. Sports can teach us a lot about determination, about goals, and, of course, about hard work.

I claim hard work and a competitive personality, which never accepts mediocrity, to be the keys to my success, and I truly believe they are. But there came a day—after I had gone to the Olympics, after I had won gold medals, after I had broken numerous records—when I found it difficult to push myself as I had in the past. Finding the kick to continue working so hard became a struggle. Yes, I still wanted to be the best swimmer I could be, but in truth the commitment just wasn't there. I was simply going through the motions: not training as hard, not watching my weight, and my mental attitude was not as tough. I tried for a while to turn things around, but when it did not happen, when I found my confidence limp as I stood behind the starting blocks, I knew it was time to hang up my suit.

I don't regret retiring. I would not have been happy with mediocre showings. I looked at my retirement as an opportunity to start a new chapter in my life, to take things I had learned about willpower and hard work, about success and failure, and apply them to a different kind of challenge. I became a coach.

Sharing my knowledge and experience with actual and potential champions is a new kind of victory. To me, the next best thing to winning a gold medal is helping someone else win one.

FOLLOW YOUR

Passion

by Johnnetta B. Cole

As far back as I can remember, whenever someone asked what I wanted to be when I grew up, I would always say "A baby doctor."

Why? Well, I didn't think I wanted to go into my family's insurance company, headquartered in my hometown of Jacksonville, Florida. Plus, I knew that wanting to be a doctor impressed grownups. It was also the case that when I was a child, specializations like neurosurgery and cardiology were regarded as men's work, and not the sort of career a young girl should seek. And I definitely liked babies.

When at age fifteen I enrolled at Fisk University in an early entrance program, and when after a year there I transferred to Oberlin College, my answer to the question "What do you want to be?" remained the same (only now I knew enough to say "pediatrician"). It was the same until I fell madly in love with anthropology.

Anthropology? I hadn't a clue what it was until I found myself in the course Introduction to Cultural Anthropology. On the very first day of class my curiosity was tickled, my interest ignited by Professor George E. Simpson, who at one point began moving most rhythmically to some music unlike anything I'd ever before heard. He explained, all the while in motion, that we were listening to the music of a Jamaican religious group, and he talked about how black culture in the Caribbean and throughout the Americas carried echoes of African culture. Back in the 1950s, this was indeed a great revelation.

And this, Professor Simpson said, is what anthropologists do: study other cultures and find connections among different kinds of people. Professor Simpson made anthropology sound so wonderful that I knew then and there it was the work I wanted to do for the rest of my life.

When I returned home for the Christmas holidays, I got a kick out of telling folks that I was majoring in anthropology.

"What's *that*?" was inevitably the response, and I got a double kick out of people's expressions of astonishment as I explained what my newfound passion was all about. "Anthropology is the study of all of humankind," I would say in a very proper voice. "There are four kinds of anthropology: cultural, physical, archaeology, and linguistics. I'm going to be a cultural anthropologist—that is, the kind that studies living people in distant lands and those who live right next door to you. Physical anthropologists study our relationship to other animals, especially primates, and how we humans are as physical beings. Archaeologists study early cultures by digging up remains from the earth. And linguists study different languages all over the world." Once I finished my "rap" on anthropology, people would say, "Oh, I see!"

I went about feeling quite pleased and impressed with myself, until the day I talked with my grandfather, whom I idolized and whose approval had always been so important to me. Like others, immediately he asked, "What's *that*?"

After I explained it, not only was my grandfather not impressed, but he also laughed outright and asked: "And how in the world are you ever going to make a living doing something like that?"

My response? I broke into tears and ran for comfort to my mother.

Like my grandfather, my mother had questioned my ability to support myself as an anthropologist. However, on this day she gave me some of the best advice I have ever received. Her words were strong and clear: "If you do work that you hate, you will be miserable for the rest of your life. If this is your passion, then follow it."

I did, and being an anthropologist, though often a struggle and fraught with uncertainties, has been a source of great emotional and intellectual riches, and a source of satisfaction and fun—as I carried out fieldwork in a black church in Chicago for my master's degree . . . and in Liberia for two years for my Ph.D. . . . and later in Cuba, Haiti, the Dominican Republic, St. Croix, and other Caribbean nations. In each of these places I was especially interested in the lives of women. I also focused on issues of race and ethnicity in those Caribbean countries. As I went about learning of various cultures and traditions, I sometimes thought about the difference between the "roughing it" that my work so often entailed and how truly rough it would have been to be engaged in work I really didn't care about.

How I wish my grandfather had lived to see the extent to which I did indeed find a way to support myself. For some thirty years I taught anthropology courses to college students, never ceasing to be genuinely happy every time I entered a classroom and began the exciting process of teaching and learning (for teachers must constantly learn, too!). And writing articles and books in the field of anthropology has also been a great source of joy for me, despite the hard work involved in preparing material for publication.

In the late 1980s the possibility of a career change came into view. To my great surprise, I was informed one day that I was being considered for the presidency of Spelman College in Atlanta, Georgia. Heading up a college had never been in my dreams, but Spelman had a special significance for me as an African American woman, because it is the oldest and one of only two historically black colleges for women. And so I followed my heart.

How fortunate I was that in assuming the presidency of Spelman I did not have to totally give up being an anthropologist. While there, I taught one course in my field every spring semester—except in 1996 when I *took* a course taught by Mary Catherine Bateson.

Another good fortune was the countless occasions to counsel students about their majors and career goals, their doubts and dilemmas.

"I love psychology, but my dad says I should major in political science," one student confided.

"Mom wants me to become a dentist like she is, but I want to be an oceanographer," another one lamented.

For yet another it was: "My parents want me to be a doctor, but I want to be a poet."

"What should I do?" they all asked.

Always my answer was the same: "Follow your passion."

I asked these students to think about how it would feel getting up every morning, day in and day out, to face work that they do not like. I reminded them that for so very long women were prohibited from pursuing many kinds of jobs, and that many people in the world have few options when it comes to what they can do to make a living. Isn't it a shame, I would point out, for someone who has the luxury of options not to explore them?

And to the student who confessed that her main motivation for choosing a particular profession was because it paid big money, I told her in a strong and clear voice that just focusing on making a good living can end up meaning not having a very good life, because a lot of money (and the things it can buy) can never truly satisfy the soul.

I believe that deep down most people know what they want to be and need to be at a very early age. It shows often in the subjects you like most. It shows in the things you like to do for fun. But what if you can't name your passion? Well, you could always talk with your parents or teachers about your interests and talents and ask them what kinds of jobs make a good match.

If you know your passion, cherish it, nurture it, let it grow. If you're not so sure, don't worry. Just stay open and curious, and in time it will make itself known to you.

IT'S NOT A CRIME TO LOVE SCIENCE

by Juliann F. Willey

"Chemistry class led me to a life of crime." This has become something of a personal slogan. I could also honestly, and perhaps more accurately, say that "Science class led me to a life of crime," because it was my interest in science as a child that planted the seeds for the job I have today: Director of the Delaware State Police Crime Lab, which means I supervise a team made up of a forensic microscopist (me), a questioned-document examiner, two chemists, and a photographer.

When I was a little girl, my love for animals made me think I would one day become a veterinarian. When I got the chance to participate in hands-on science classes and labs in junior high school, I knew for sure that I wanted to grow up to work in science.

I can remember dissecting earthworms, frogs, and starfish—and not thinking, Yuck!, but rather how cool it was to find out how these creatures functioned. I can remember learning about the planets and the stars so far up above and about minerals and fossils beneath the earth's surface and thinking, Wow! What a world!

My excitement over science did nothing but grow during high school and during my college days, too—only by then I had discovered that I didn't want to be a veterinarian. My courses in analytical and organic chemistry and biochemistry helped me understand how and why things worked the way they do—from how the chemicals in perms make your hair curly to why your blood clots when you get a cut or bruise. Eventually my focus became forensics—the application of science to matters of the law. My interest in forensics had actually been sparked a few years earlier by the television series *Quincy, M.E.,* which starred Jack Klugman as a feisty medical examiner who helped the Los Angeles County police department solve crimes.

Eventually I became a forensic microscopist, and with my three trusty Olympus microscopes I assist in crime-busting by analyzing what we call "known" items (like head hairs or clothing fibers from a victim) and "questioned" items (things collected at the scene of a crime, such as vacuum sweepings and suspects' clothing). The results of my examination are then handed over to the investigating officer—to be used in tracking down a criminal or proving the innocence of a suspect.

Given what I do for a living, when I spot something harmful, hurtful, and just plain wrong, I tend to view it as a crime. One of the crimes I've been scoping out for a while is the discouragement of girls from studying the sciences—a surefire method of scaring many away from ever at least considering a career in the field.

And it's a serial crime, taking place all across the nation, affecting girl after girl, day after day. When I contemplate what can be done about it, I can't help but fall back on the procedures I use in my work.

So I've looked at the "known" items—information found in various studies—which include:

- **Girls are not being encouraged to take science class.**
- **Boys and girls are not being treated equally in many classrooms.**
- **Different expectations are placed on boys than on girls.**

As for the "questioned" items, traces of strange ideas have been found again and again at the scenes of the crime. Among them:

1. A person who loves science class is *definitely* uncool.
2. Having a passion for science will have you doing *nothing* but homework, with no time for fun.
3. The *worst* thing a girl can do is show her "mental muscles"—especially in front of boys.
4. Anyone who pursues a career in the sciences will end up in some *boring* job in some *boring* lab in some *boring* company somewhere.

My analysis strongly suggests that the prime suspects are Stereotypes and Ignorance, repeat offenders that have been around for a very long time, clogging girls' heads with a lot of nonsense, a lot of lies. They've even got some parents, teachers, and guidance counselors serving as their accomplices—sometimes willingly and often unwittingly—when, for example, they discourage girls from adventures in something like carpentry or auto mechanics. What's more, the culprits have operatives in the entertainment and advertising industries who put out the vile message that a female's sole purpose in life is to be beautiful.

What's to be done? I can't think of anything more necessary than a big dose of truth.

1. There's nothing more uncool than letting other people keep you from the positive things you enjoy.
2. If you run across a science maniac who's all work and no play, trust me, it's a personality thing. It's not biology or chemistry class that has made this person antisocial and one-dimensional. I am living proof that you can be serious about science and have fun. In high school I ran varsity cross-country, played varsity basketball, participated in various clubs, and went out with friends.
3. The *worst* thing a girl can do is hide her mental muscles—in front of anyone! Not that you should show off your smarts, but it's foolish to camouflage it, because the kinds of people who are worth your while are the kinds of people who respect, admire, and rejoice at intelli-

gence. Those who are intimidated by a smart girl are *definitely* bad news. In the long run, their insecurity will only pull you down and hold you back.

4. The range of jobs in the world of science is awesome. There is something in the field for all kinds of personalities and interests. Science class could lead to a life of healing (a doctor), a life of improving our eating (nutritionist), a life of probing and protecting our world (astronomer, geologist, zoologist, marine biologist, environmental scientist), and so many other careers. When it comes to a job in which a lab is the primary work site, the fact of the matter is that fascinating things go on in labs, and there's really little room for boredom. Think of the challenges facing our world today, such as finding cures for cancer, AIDS, and other diseases; creating vegetable plants that generate high-yield, robust produce; developing materials and products that are functional yet biodegradable. This is the kind of work that goes on in labs. Of course, if you're into justice and a safer nation, you could always become a forensic scientist like me.

Surely more teachers, parents, and other adults need to step up and join the science awareness patrol by, for example, buying a chemistry set as well as a tea set for a girl who's shown an interest and aptitude for science; by not making a girl feel that a life in the sciences is off-limits to her merely because she is female.

Such tactics have tremendous value, but it's also vital for girls to take preventive measures to avoid becoming a victim of the crime, by saying no to Stereotypes and Ignorance, by holding up the truth.

And the world will become a more welcoming place for girls who want to say yes to the sciences.

8

Envision

by Vera Wang

I believe that my lifelong infatuation with fashion really coincided with my childhood passion for figure skating. For me, these two worlds would always be inextricably intertwined. Skating was one of the most joyous and exhilarating experiences I could have ever imagined—flying over the ice, emoting to all kinds of music, feeling the autonomy and freedom of my own body—it was positively heaven! And almost from the start, skating dresses became an integral part of that experience: designing them, fitting them, creating a vision all my own and one that would only serve to enhance my skating performances. What a wonderful and creative means it was to incorporate a love of athletics with the worlds of dance, music, and fashion.

By the time I entered secondary school I was already deeply ensconced in the grueling world of amateur competition, which continued all the way through my freshman year at Sarah Lawrence College. In 1968, however, failing to qualify for the United States Olympic Team, I decided to quit competitive skating forever. This would prove to be a difficult and painful decision for me and result in a strange and confusing period in my life. Without a degree in fashion design, and anxious to fill the creative void that skating had left, I eventually started, after my graduation from college, as an editorial assistant at *Vogue* magazine, and hoped that this first step would ultimately lead to a design job for me somewhere down the road.

Little did I know then that I was to spend the next fifteen years at

Vogue, ultimately as a senior fashion editor. I began at the very bottom, photocopying petty-cash receipts, filling out messenger slips, and helping to pack and unpack clothing brought in for editorial meetings. In the end, however, nothing could compare with the training I received as a *Vogue* "sittings" editor. By styling the fashion pages of the magazine, I was in a very real position to create and promote trends and, ultimately, to influence

thousands of women. It was both a privilege and a responsibility, and beyond all else, an opportunity to work with some very gifted people: photographers, hair stylists, makeup artists, and, of course, designers.

When eventually I did move on from *Vogue,* it was to pursue my much-belated dream of becoming a designer. I ended up securing a challenging and multi-faceted job as one of the design directors at Ralph Lauren. As was true at *Vogue,* this was to be a place where only the highest levels of taste, talent, and commitment were tolerated.

For quite some time I had harbored the idea of starting my own fashion company. With limited financial and human resources, however, I realized very early on that I had to keep my focus extremely narrow if I was to succeed. Bridal dresses appealed to me because, as a fashion insider, and as a recent bride, I realized the void that existed in the bridal market for modern, minimal, and sophisticated wedding dresses. Here was an incredible opportunity for me to utilize all my styling expertise and design vision in an area that had been virtually ignored by the rest of the fashion world. If I could create a new and different perception of bridal style (*and noticeably distinguish myself and my "look" from the pack*), then perhaps I could lay the foundation for a serious fashion company.

The first step was to create a direct relationship with my client. By opening my own shop, Vera Wang Bridal House, I was able to convey my own sense of taste and control both the image and merchandising of my store. I was also capable of studying which dresses most appealed to

my customers, which shapes were truly flattering, and which price points my customers really could afford. For me, it was also *not* simply about selling a dress but about providing the best quality, the best styling, and a true sense of individuality for my client.

Establishing my second division, Vera Wang Made-to-Order, accomplished many other things. First and foremost it gave me the rarefied opportunity to closely study the lost art of couture dressmaking dress by dress, and to work with fabrics too precious and expensive to use in ready-to-wear lines. It also enabled me to provide, as a special service to my clients, one-of-a-kind dresses of extraordinary quality and custom designed for those determined to have nothing less than the "couture" experience. Special design projects, such as my dresses for Olympian Nancy Kerrigan or such Hollywood celebrities as Sharon Stone or Holly Hunter, were also created in my couture workroom by couture hands.

Thanks in part to the incredible publicity my clothes have generated, it seems perhaps as if this has all been somewhat effortless. Nothing, however, could be further from the truth. I was being called upon to deal with each and every element of running my own company, from cash-flow analyses and sales projections to working capital and employee benefits. The decisions I made on a daily basis had to keep pace with the ever-mounting problems. Limited real estate and tight budgets were just some of the major obstacles that I had to learn to coexist with. Despite these incredible odds, however, my ultimate reward has been the reality that I am doing my own thing, for better or worse. Any subsequent success or failure will be of my own accord, but at least for the moment I am totally satisfied. I will have given myself a shot at what I have always loved doing most: designing, and designing my own way.

What, one may ask, prompted me to make such an enormous shift from dedicated employee to "fearless" entrepreneur? Perhaps the answer to my story is as simple as a vision of a little girl skating all alone on a sheet of ice—free, and happy, with a fierce love of independence.

SOME SOLITUDE IS GOOD

by Mary Catherine Bateson

Alone. It's a sad sort of word, whether we're talking about an afternoon or a year. Many people, if they find themselves alone for a time, quick-quick get on the telephone or turn up the volume on the TV to drown out their own thoughts. Anything, they think, is better than nothing.

A lot of girls are taught to feel vulnerable when they are alone, even at home. A lot of girls grow up expecting to find fulfillment only in being with others.

But being *alone* is part of being *your own:* your own person, your own best friend. Being alone is not the same as being helpless or abandoned or incomplete unless you choose to make it so.

Often enough your own spirit is the best company you can find. Often, too, the companionship chosen just to avoid solitude offers danger or damage.

I've known teenagers who hang out with others they don't really respect or trust, just to have someone to hang out with, just not to feel like an outsider. I've known young women who stay with abuse, getting beaten up again and again, because they just can't imagine being on their own. I've known middle-aged women who have so lost themselves in the role of wife or mother that if there's a divorce, or when the children leave the nest, or a partner of many years dies, they have to learn from scratch how to cope and how to enjoy their solitude.

It's worth learning early on how to be alone, how to treasure solitude, and how to fill your solitude with imagined friends and adventures. No one can laugh at your private yearnings and daydreams.

In the city you can find places where it is safe to walk or where you can sit quietly, churches that are kept open, libraries, or museums that don't charge admission.

Trees and waves make good company.

Birdsong is an enhancement of silence.

In a crowded apartment, you can learn to withdraw in the presence of others.

A lot of deep thoughts have occurred while washing dishes or peeling potatoes.

Rocking a baby sister or brother to sleep or singing lullabies can offer quiet and peace to weep or chuckle about the day.

"I'm doing my homework" should include "*I'm thinking* about my homework," or my project, or something the teacher said in class. There is a direct connection between the capacity to withdraw and reflect and success in school and work. *I'm just thinking* is part of learning, of being human.

Adults are concerned about making sure that young people are not left alone where this would be dangerous, and habits linger on. Just as you need to learn first to tolerate and then to enjoy solitude, you need to show that you can be trusted to use solitude responsibly. There is a lot to be said for seeking the opportunity to go away to camp or school, visiting relatives out of town and entering a community of strangers by yourself, or one day getting a job in an unfamiliar city or joining the military. Stay with it even if you are homesick. Let the homesickness teach you about love for family—and about your own ability to settle in and feel at home elsewhere, to build a home for yourself and others.

Loneliness can be painful, but it can teach you, too. Use it to discover new possibilities within you and how much you can do for yourself. Sometimes being alone can make you feel helpless and incompetent, so learn how to change a fuse or a tire, how to do simple first aid. How to find and keep a job. Being your own person is knowing that you can make it on your own.

Learning to be alone should not turn you into a loner. Savoring solitude actually frees you up for love and caring—by showing you that companionship is your own choice. And even when you find others with whom you are happy, save some time for solitude: for dreaming, planning, and remembering, for rediscovering your own tempo and your own strength.

10

DON'T FAST-FORWARD
by Joyce A. Ladner

Dear Sonia,

I have often thought about you since you spent last summer with me. We had such fun touring the White House. The trip to the National Zoo reminded me of how small the zoo is in Hattiesburg, with its one elephant. Your tumble of questions after our visits to the Washington Monument and the Lincoln Memorial reminded me very much of my high school history classes (only your questions had a lot more edge). And I still remember the look of excitement on your face when you first laid eyes on Howard University. I hope that when the time comes for you to go to college that it'll at least be among your top picks.

Some of the friends you made in the summer science program at Howard called to ask if I had heard from you lately. They asked me to tell you "hi" when I did, and a few asked for your address. And I saw your math teacher recently. She sang your praises and talked about how much she enjoyed teaching you and how superb you are in math.

Even though we had a lot of fun over the summer, you and I did not always get along. You kept wanting to listen to music with the volume turned to Loud, and I kept at you to turn the radio down. I have to admit, your grandmother told me to turn the radio down (a lot!) when I was your age. (So don't be surprised if in twenty or thirty years you find yourself fussing at some young person about her music being too loud.)

You also said I was too strict.

You wanted to know why you couldn't go to the movies and to parties with your cousins who are practically grown. You

cried buckets and said I didn't trust you. And I haven't
forgotten the time I wouldn't let you talk to that boy who
called at eleven P.M. You didn't want to go to your classes
the next day because you said you couldn't face him and your
friends.

"You treat me like a baby!" I believe those were your
words. How my heart sank when you put that sign on your bed-
room door: DO NOT ENTER WITHOUT PERMISSION!

Maybe this letter can explain why I treated you as I did,
why I "watched you like a hawk," as you put it.

Sonia, I am not a "mean" person who wanted you to have a
miserable summer vacation, but when I saw that you were so
on fire to grow up fast, I had to do what I believed to be
right. I did what I did because I don't want you to see the
troubles that can come when you rush after all the privi-
leges of being grown before you have a clue about the
responsibilities that come with the territory. I did what I
did because I love you.

I want you to enjoy your life without the burdens that
come with growing up too soon. I want you to have an opportunity to daydream about what you want to be when you grow
up. I want you to be carefree, even as you learn how to
gradually handle responsibility. I want to protect you even
as I encourage you to mature, to grow, to fly.

You cannot expect to grow up overnight. We grow and mature
in stages. Can you remember what you were like when you were
six years old? Ten years old? You were very different then
than you are now, right? Well, you will be different at fourteen, sixteen, eighteen, and twenty-one. You shouldn't treat
life like you do a video when you hit what you feel is a dull
part: You shouldn't try to fast-forward yourself.

Adolescence is a time for trying on different personalities until you find one that fits you. It's similar to going
into a store and trying on different brands of jeans until
you find the pair that fits just right. But even as you test
the limits the adults have set for you, and flesh out your

personality, you will also continue to change with each passing day. That, in a nutshell, is what I mean about how important it is for you to give yourself the time and the breathing room *to be!*

When I was fifteen, one of my classmates got pregnant and had a baby. She hadn't listened to her parents when they told her not to date a boy who was eighteen, because he was too worldly for her, and he was about to join the army. After she had the baby, her parents made her quit school and stay home to take care of her child. Her boyfriend went into the army and started dating someone else. He gave my friend no help with their baby.

My friend was sad and angry that she couldn't go to the movies and to basketball games with her friends. The baby took up a lot of her time—time she used to spend being care-free and having fun. Once, she believed that having a boyfriend—and an older guy at that—would cause us girls to envy her. And she was right, for in the beginning we thought she was hip because a handsome, almost-grown man asked her to date him. But soon our envy turned to something like pity.

She never went back to school, and she went on to make a series of bad decisions that forced her to grow up quicker than she should have and in ways she'd never imagined. She missed out on a lot of opportunities, a lot of the good things in life. Years later even she said she made a big mistake by not listening to her parents. And there was no way for her to rewind. I never want you to have to wish you could rewind.

Sonia, just as you've had only one childhood, you will have only one go-round as an adolescent. Enjoy just being a teenager now! After you hit eighteen, you'll have decades— your whole lifetime—to do grown-up things.

Please believe me when I say that I love you very, very much. And here's hoping you'll come to see me again next summer.

       Love,
       Aunt Joyce

SOME DREAMS ARE NIGHTMARES

by Ann Decker

50

© ANN DECKER 1997

look far and high

An interview with Lauren Hutton

Q: YOU'VE HAD A VERY SUCCESSFUL CAREER AS A MODEL, AND IT'S WIDELY KNOWN THAT YOU AREN'T VAIN. HOW COME?

A: Let's qualify that. If you've lived by looks all your adult life, you're probably a lot vainer than you think. *But,* as a kid I was extremely skinny, made fun of, not popular, *and* had no dates! And there were six things in the backyard that could kill you, besides my stepfather. That alone can keep you too busy to look in a mirror. Also, when I was growing up I was told all the time that beauty's only skin deep. And I had an example: My mother was *extremely* beautiful, whereas my aunt with whom we lived for a while in Miami, though not really plain, was certainly no serious knockdown beauty like my mother. But it was my aunt who had the time to listen to me and treat me as an individual. So, to me, my aunt was much more beautiful. There was no comparison between the beauty of these two women. It helped give me real eyes. And that was just the physical side of it.

On top of not being a "beautiful" girl, there were much more interesting things going on in my life—like poverty. Although my mother had come from a "nice" bourgeois family in Charleston, South Carolina, by the time I was six we were very poor. My mother's second husband was a spirited man, an adventurous man who had lived in the Amazon and had just come out of the oil fields of Venezuela when he met my mother. But almost immediately after they married he lost the money he'd saved and what money my mother had inherited. So we ended up poor on the edge of a swamp outside Tampa, Florida. The things, besides my stepdad, that could kill you were six-foot diamondback rattlesnakes, water moccasins, copperheads, coral snakes, and alligators. And there were always roving gangs of boys since there was a strict no-girls-in-the-woods law—but I was a lawbreaker.

Then by the time I was thirteen my mother was very ill. She had three other children—one just born, one eleven months old, and one five. So I, the oldest by far, became nanny, cook, maid, mother. I became a one-skinny-girl workforce, also trying to keep up with high school. A savage but character-building experience. My mother and my stepfather were both practicing alcoholics by now. This added to the weekend emergency room trips and to one of my other household duties, fight referee. So as a child and as a teenager I certainly knew what pain was. And suffering . . .

that can make a philosopher of you. If you're going to live through it, if you're going to come out on the other side laughing and with some sense of optimism, you've got to learn to look far and high. Years later an Arab girlfriend in Morocco taught me this while teaching me to ride Arabian stallions: "If you look down to the ground, you'll fall. But if you look far and high, you'll fly."

You must figure out that in this one quick life you've only got a certain amount of time. Do you want to waste it with your lip poked out about what your mom and stepdad did and what you had to go through? Or look past the ugly stuff to what you want your life to look like? If you have some idea of what you like and what you want, you'll know where to aim and chances are you'll get it. I did. With no help but my own wit.

Q: WHAT HELPED YOU ENDURE?

A: First, nature. And second, books. And somewhere between, laughing with my baby sisters and wanting to protect them.

The outdoors was just always my favorite beauty place and my saving grace. Some little patch of wild grass can restore. When things were really, really impossible, I'd go outside and sit at the edge of our swamp. If it was night, I'd go out and just lie there. I'd be looking up at the stars . . . so many stars, so many planets, so many creatures, so many creatures' families . . . Pretty soon everything—my problems, my family's crises—would disappear into space. Living out in the woods was in so many ways a real strengthening. It taught me to watch. It taught me to be quiet and to have patience. If I wasn't observant I might step on a rattlesnake or a three-hundred-pound alligator might get me. If I didn't have patience I wouldn't be able to catch a fish—and I fished a lot!

The other thing I discovered is that anything there is to learn in the world you can learn in nature, from design to taste to reason to philosophy. Anything, everything, can be learned if you can just get yourself in a little patch of real ground, real nature, real woods, real anything, any corner of a man-made garden or park—and just sit still and watch. As long as there are bugs and plants and nature, you get to see God's face there, no question about it. The time that I spent like that is the reason I've traveled so much in the last twenty-five years, especially to Africa, Asia, and South America. I'm involved in environmental organizations because I've seen so many places destroyed, village after village, town after town.

Q: WHAT ELSE HAS HELPED YOU GROW?

A: Reading. I didn't learn to read until I was twelve years old. Because I had a big memory and vocabulary, I was able to fake my way through till fourth grade. When I was busted and finally did start reading I did it with a vengeance. Everybody who has had something to say pretty much in the history of the world has got it down somewhere, and you can talk to all those people. You can listen to them and get all their information. I go out to dinner by myself with a book all the time. I used to get a little nervous when I was in my twenties, because people would recognize me. I'd think, Maybe they think I can't get a date. "Lauren Hutton, what's she doing alone?" Boy, I am sure not self-conscious anymore. I can be having an unbelievable conversation with a book and having the most fine time alone. In fact, I much prefer to be alone than with dull company.

Q: HAVE YOU BECOME THE WOMAN YOU HOPED TO BECOME WHEN YOU WERE A GIRL?

A: I think you spend your whole life doing that. It takes a long time just to find what it is that you really want, as opposed to what your family wants, what your friends want, and what all these people—what current society—thinks you should want. Society is a herd of sheep. What they think is always changing, as soon as somebody smart tells them different. Like when I said, "Hey, half of America is over forty-five and half are women, how about some models over thirty?" In eighty years of American magazines this was a brand-new idea, and once they got this new idea, society changed. That's one reason I am always encouraging young people to hold on to their curiosity and to find their particular, unique way to change the thinking of the world. One of the things I was told all the time when I was a kid was "You've got too much imagination, girl," or "Your imagination's running away with you!" Adults often don't understand a lot of things about kids. We often crush some of the most precious things. But if you can hold on to your curiosity, you'll have a better chance of finding yourself: who you are, what you want, and what you want to be—right now, tomorrow, ten years from now, forever.

THE WIDER YOUR TIRES, THE BETTER

by Kyoko Mori

When I was thirteen, I wrote letters to myself in the future and sealed them in envelopes addressed:

> *To Kyoko at eighteen . . .*
> *To Kyoko at twenty . . .*
> *To Kyoko at twenty-five . . .*

They were to be opened on the birthdays when I reached those ages.

Now that I am forty, I have forgotten what I did with the letters after opening them on the appointed day—eighteen and twenty in my father's house in Japan . . . twenty-five in my studio apartment in Milwaukee, Wisconsin, where I was attending graduate school. Amused by the earnest tone of the letters, I put them aside. But I still remember some of the messages repeated in each letter.

Wherever you are, I hope you are doing what makes you happy. If things are not going your way, if you have not yet achieved everything you wanted, please remember that I wished you the best and had so much hope for you—don't be discouraged. I hope you are still working hard to become a writer or an artist.

What motivated me to write those letters was worry. At thirteen I was afraid of growing up. By the time I became a full-grown woman, I feared, I might have abandoned everything that was once so important to me: becoming a writer or an artist, holding on to my ambition, being true to my sense of happiness and integrity. I had good reason to be worried. What I was hearing about "becoming a woman" didn't sound very attractive. From the health teacher who told us about menstruation to the home economics teacher who drilled us on how to plan nutritious meals for our future families, everyone was telling us that someday we would get married, have children, and devote ourselves to making our husbands and children happy.

The few girls in my class who had boyfriends were fine with this. They talked and behaved as though their boyfriends were everything and they themselves were nothing. These girls were constantly concerned with being pretty enough and nice enough for the boys.

We were going to a private all-girls junior high school in Nishinomiya, a suburb of Kobe in Japan. During school hours my friends were smart, ambitious, competitive. They seemed to value (as I did) their own talents and achievements: We all prided ourselves on getting good grades in every subject, and on being fast runners, powerful shot-putters, or good basketball players. We competed in foot races and in writing contests, too. Our friendships were based on competition and mutual respect.

If I could have seen my friends only during school hours, when there were no boys around, I would have had nothing to worry about. But outside of school my friends became different. On the commuter train taking us home, or in the stores in downtown Kobe on weekends, I hardly recognized them. In the presence of boys my friends began to whisper and giggle instead of speaking up clearly. On the train some would sigh and crumple down into their seats as though the books and shopping bags they carried were too heavy for their delicate shoulders to bear. No one would believe that these were the same girls who swam fifty-meter butterfly races and projected their voices to the back row of the auditorium in speech contests.

When I pointed out the silliness of their behavior, my friends frowned and hissed, "You are such a child. Wait till you see a boy you like, even if he takes no notice of you. Then you, too, will start acting more like a woman instead of a tomboy."

Their words sounded like a fairy-tale curse: "When you grow up, you will prick your finger and fall asleep for a hundred years. You will turn into a bat and fly around for centuries, silly and giggly." The future looked dismal. I wrote the letters to an older Kyoko as an incantation against such a spell.

Apparently it worked. I did not become a silly woman, prone to giggling or whispering and playing frail when toting heavy bags. I write, teach, run six days a week, lift weights, and ride my bicycle. And I have many male friends. When we are working or running or hanging out together, we don't focus on our male-female difference, because it's completely irrelevant to what we are doing.

The first time I noticed that my male friends treat me the same as they treat each other, I was a graduate student in Milwaukee. I had been running for about a year with a group of friends, all of whom were men. I went to watch them compete in a ten-kilometer race I was unable to run because I had sprained an ankle a few weeks earlier. I arrived on my bicycle, parked for the start, and then rode to the first-, third-, and fourth-mile marks. I saw most of my friends running past the mile marks, shouted the kinds of things runners say to each other—"Looking good" . . . "Nice pace. Keep it up" . . . "Swing those arms"—and then I headed toward the finish line.

About twenty yards from the finish line I saw one of my running buddies, Jeff. He was standing alone, surrounded by other onlookers, all of whom were women.

It had been cloudy all morning. Now it started to drizzle. Jeff and I traded stories about our injuries (he had shin splints) and our comeback plans. Then we discussed which runners were doing well at the mile marks and who was struggling.

By the time the first few runners came into view, it was raining steadily. We didn't expect our friends to be among the first five or six, who were running four-minute miles. The fastest of our friends, Mark, ran five-and-a-half-minute miles and would be in the second wave of runners.

While Jeff and I squinted in the rain, looking for Mark's blue singlet and black shorts, the area around the finish line filled up with tremendous noise. All around us women were screaming their husbands' and boyfriends' names, jumping up and down, and running to the line where the runners stood breathing hard. The women whose men hadn't come in yet stared down the street with forlorn faces. Most of them, without umbrellas, were clutching towels, a change of clothes, and oranges or bananas for their men. Shoulders hunched, the women pressed these things against their chests to keep them dry. Somehow the sight depressed me.

"Hey." Jeff nudged me. "Let's walk down a block."

I could scarcely hear him because of all the screaming. The second wave of runners was coming in now.

"Let's get away from these women," Jeff urged, his voice pitched louder now.

"Yeah," I agreed. "Good idea."

Halfway down the block we spotted Mark running five steps ahead of another runner and trying to shake him off.

"Last block!" Jeff called out. "Move it! Don't let him pass you!"

"Sprint!" I shouted. "Give it all you've got!"

In the next few minutes we saw most of our friends going through the finish line: Bob, Brooks, Fred, Ray, Bill, Alan . . .

Everyone was coming in about thirty or sixty seconds behind their best ten-kilometer times. Maybe the course was harder than expected; maybe the rain had distracted them.

"Those guys," Jeff said, shaking his head. "They can't do their best without us pushing them."

"Yeah," I said. "We'd better get over these injuries pretty quick."

We weren't being arrogant. In the group we trained with, Jeff and I were in the middle pack in terms of ability. There were a couple of runners we could never beat, and a couple we could always beat. Competition made all of us run faster. Jeff and I were both known for starting out fast and finishing with a strong kick. Our friends counted on us to push them at the beginning and at the end. We relied on them to keep us going in between.

After the last of our friends came through, Jeff and I didn't join them at the finish line. We figured they'd have sense enough to head straight for the gym, change into dry clothes, and go home before they caught a cold. There would be plenty of time to talk about the race once we were back training with them. So Jeff, who lived nearby, headed home on foot, and I got back on my bicycle. It was a cheap, heavy bike I had bought second-hand. One good thing: The tires were wide, so I could ride in the rain.

On the way home I realized how Jeff had talked about "the guys" to mean our fellow runners and "the women" to mean the screaming onlook-ers. According to those definitions, I was more a guy than a woman. And that was all right by me.

If I could write back to the thirteen-year-old I used to be, I would thank her for all her worries, concerns, and hopes, but I would thank her even more for running. Running has been the foundation for so many things in my life: cycling, swimming, weightlifting—and the confidence all these activities have inspired. Running has also taught me that the alleged man-woman differences are often smaller than the differences between one man and another man, between one woman and another woman. There are men who run a little faster than I and men who run a little slower than I—but there are women who run much faster than the men who run a little faster than I.

"It must be so hard to be the only woman in your department. I would hate to work with all those men." I've heard this many times, I'm sorry to say, from other women, because at the college where I teach, I happen to be the only full-time woman English professor. True, every time we have a departmental meeting, and I am sitting in a room with eight male profes-sors, I wish I were not the only woman in my department, but that's because I know the importance of role models. At my college about half the students are women, so it would be better if the teachers, too, were divided more equally between men and women. Our women students deserve to see other women in positions of authority and respect. It would boost their confidence, I am sure. But as for myself, I don't feel singled out or intimidated by my male colleagues. In fact, two of the men I work with are among the closest friends I have ever had in my life. We often run together and have long talks about work, family, books, ideas.

People have to get over the idea that men and women are complete opposites, that we can never be similar. Those who assume the worst seem to believe in all the old stereotypes: men are competitive, aggressive, rational (and run faster and do better in school), while women seek peace and cooperation, value intuition and emotion (and cook better and know what colors match).

Notions such as these only hinder us. For men and women alike, there are times when we should be competitive, confrontational, intellectual, and there are times when we should seek compromise, cooperation, and listen to our emotions. Most situations call for a blend of all of the above, and most men and women have the ability to be all of these things. It's wrong to assume that these ways of being are gender-bound—as though at the moment of our birth mean fairies bestow upon us a curse disguised as a blessing, saying to the girl-child: "You will be kind but irrational," and to the boy-child: "You will be smart but unsympathetic."

I don't want a mixed blessing. I want to run fast and be able to sit still for hours of writing. I want to construct a logical argument for what I believe with all my feelings. I want to be smart, competitive, and kind.

I am not ashamed of being a woman. I know I am a woman twenty-four hours a day, just as I know that all the day long I am a Japanese-American, right-handed, and five foot three inches tall.

At thirteen I didn't want to grow up to be a woman because I thought being a woman meant playing feminine-dumb and giving up my ambitions to make some man happy. I didn't realize that becoming a grown woman could also include becoming intelligent, hardworking, athletic, independent, compassionate, and every glorious thing I wanted to be. If I could write a letter to the thirteen-year-old me I would tell her:

Don't worry. Your friends are wrong to say that you are childish and immature because you don't want to become "a woman." Most of them will get over that silly way of being a woman. You will have your smart girlfriends back in a few years, as well as new friends, men and women both. Thank you for worrying about me. I am happy.

say *what you*

DON'T
WANT

14

by Deborah Tannen

Girls say boys are mean, and boys say girls talk about every little thing forever—and it's hard to know what they really mean. Where do these attitudes come from, and what are their consequences?

These attitudes come, at least partly, from differences in the way girls
and boys learn to play with their friends as children. Although there are
always some girls who prefer to play with boys, and some boys who would
rather play with girls, most children spend most of their time playing with
other children of the same gender, and boys and girls tend not to play the
same ways. As a result, older girls and boys (and, later, women and men)
can have very different ways of communicating and interacting. This can
be frustrating for both. In some cases it can be dangerous for girls.

A while back I taught a course to college students on the ways that
boys and girls and women and men use language. I asked my students to
keep a log of their own experiences that related to the course. One young

man, Anthony Marchese, wrote about playing Jenga, a game of blocks, with two friends:

We played about three or four games, and then we started building things with the blocks. It was really fun because we felt like little kids again. There were three of us building our own little structures, two guys and one girl, Alicia. We had each built a unique design when suddenly the other guy threw a block at my structure to knock it over. It only glanced my building, and for the most part it stayed up. I then threw a block at his building, which prompted him to throw a block at Alicia's. She put her arms around her building to shield it from the flying blocks. While my friend and I destroyed each other's buildings, we couldn't get hers because we did not want to hit her with the blocks. Another guy in the room said to her, "Why didn't you throw blocks at them?" She said she did not like to play that way and she did not find our play very amusing. I did not want my building ruined, but I had a lot of fun throwing blocks at my friend's and destroying his.

Anthony realized he was playing the way he had played as a child. Part of the fun was building his own structure, but another part was destroying someone else's. Anthony and the other young man had the same idea of what was fun, but Alicia did not share that idea. Anthony guessed (correctly, I think) that when Alicia was a little girl, having fun with friends didn't include destroying each other's creations. This partly explains why when boys and girls try to play together, girls often end up thinking boys are mean.

Now, what about boys' attitude that girls talk on and on about insignificant things, and that it's hard to know what they're getting at?

Another one of my students, Aiyana Hoffman, took several classmates to her twelve-year-old cousin's birthday party. At one point there was a lot of commotion at the party because one girl (I'll call her Mary) said something that hurt the feelings of another girl (I'll call her Sue). Sue felt so bad, she went into the bathroom, crying. Immediately the other girls were going in and out of the bathroom to check on Sue, to find out what was wrong and try to make her feel better. Sue's best friend (Kate) seemed to be in charge, speaking privately with all the other girls, reporting on Sue's feelings and even talking privately with Mary—the girl who had hurt Sue's feelings.

While the girls were caught up in this drama, the boys were playing video games and, as my student Cortney Howard put it, "goofing off." One boy (I'll call him Jason) was giving another boy (Joe) a hard time, and two other boys joined in. Their conversation (which Cortney wrote down) went like this:

JASON: So what's up with Karen? She's got you all whooped.

JOE: No, dude, she's just some girl, nothin' special. I ain't whooped.

JASON: Yeah, you've been calling her. I saw you talking to her on the playground after school last week, too.

JOE: What are you talking about? I was just getting the math homework, that's all.

JASON: Horse crap! You like her!

SAM: Look, man, he's turning red! You're turning red! Ha-ha!

JACK: You wimp, you're red all over that ugly face of yours!

This conversation is different from the girls' in many ways. First of all, Jason insulted Joe openly, and the other boys joined in. When Mary said something to make Sue feel bad, she said it in private, and the other girls only found out later what it was. When they did, they tried to console her.

And did you notice how the boys and girls reacted differently when their friends showed their feelings? When Joe turned red, it became another reason for the other boys to put him down—to call him a wimp. Sue didn't hide her hurt. It gave her a kind of power when she cried in the bathroom. In a way she became the most important person at the party, and the bathroom became her headquarters! My students also noticed another difference between the boys and the girls at the party. When they came upon Kate and Mary whispering in the laundry room, the girls immediately stopped talking, not wanting strangers to overhear their secrets. But when the college students were listening in on Jason and his buddies, the boys "kind of acted up," as my student wrote, "as if they were playing in front of an important audience." This made me think about how many girls are reluctant to talk in front of others—for example, in class, where many boys actually compete to be called on, stretching out their arms and even waving them or calling out.

The girls' way of negotiating their friendships and rivalries was done in private conversations, but the boys' way emphasized showmanship, which has to be done with an audience. Because the boys are used to playing out their rivalries publicly, they don't know what to make of conversations like the girls at the party were having in the bathroom and the laundry room. That explains, at least partly, why the boys think the girls go on and on about unimportant things. What's important to the girls—conversations about who said what to whom and how that made them feel—seems unimportant to the boys.

These two examples can help us understand what happens when boys and girls get together. At the birthday party the boys and girls tended to play separately, even though they were all at the same gathering. But when boys and girls get older, they spend more and more time together, either in groups or in pairs. Like the college students playing Jenga, they have different ideas of how to do things together and how to talk about what they want, and this makes things awkward or even dangerous, especially if the boys want to do something that the girls don't want to do.

When Anthony and his friend wanted to throw blocks and destroy each other's buildings, but Alicia didn't want to, she protected her building by shielding it with her arms. But it isn't always that simple. What if a boy wants to do something that has to do with sex and the girl doesn't want to? In a book called *The Difference,* Judy Mann tells about a study that really made me think. Two researchers named Marion Howard and Judith McCabe asked more than a thousand sexually active girls what they most wanted to have more information about. Rather than checking off contraception or the mechanics of sex, eighty-four percent checked this: "How to say no without hurting the other person's feelings."

If a boy wants a girl to do something she doesn't want to do, this is what can happen: While she is trying to balance what she wants with her concern about his feelings and what he wants, he is concentrating only on what he wants and assumes that she will concentrate on what she wants. This imbalance is what can be dangerous. She probably doesn't realize that he is working by a different system, so she thinks that if she gives him a hint that she doesn't want to do something, he will pick up the hint and back off—without his feelings getting hurt. But if he isn't used to communicating that way, he won't be listening for hints. The result can be that she does something she doesn't want to do, and he may never realize how much she didn't want to do it.

This might sound like another way of saying that boys are mean, that they're selfish and just go after what they want. But you don't have to look at it that way. If two people get together, and each one looks out for himself or herself, it's a fair situation—the kind of situation most boys are used to, because that's the way they've been playing all their lives.

Think back to the birthday party. Remember how Sue's hurt feelings gave her so much power because all the girls were concerned with her feelings? That shows how girls learn, from early on, to pay a lot of attention to others' feelings. When Joe showed his feelings by blushing, the other boys used it against him, calling him a wimp. That shows how boys learn to hide or deny feelings rather than pay extra attention to them.

Once girls understand the different ways that boys and girls interact, they should feel free to concentrate on what they want or don't want.

And make it clear.

And insist on it.

It's fairer to themselves, and it's fairer to the boys, who often don't realize what girls are getting at when they try to say no without hurting boys' feelings.

15 aren't always lost

by Sharon Creech

THURSDAY, JULY 5

Today was interesting (for a change). . . .

Where shall I begin. . . ?

Sure enough, Alex Cheevey was at the pool again. . . .

First we practiced diving. We were giving each other numbers (you know, like 10, 9, 8, etc.) for the quality of our dives. Then we started goofing around and doing clown dives and acting stupid. . . .

When the next break was called, he said, "Hey, let's leave." Did you catch that? He said "Let's" as in "Let *us*"! He wanted me to leave *with* him.

Then he walked me *home*. He didn't hang around because he had to go to work. He works part-time for a landscaping company, mowing lawns and pulling weeds and trimming bushes. Anyway, he said he had to work all day on Friday and Saturday, but, but, but, Alex Cheevey actually asked me if I wanted to go swimming again on Sunday! I mean he didn't just say, "Are you going to be at the pool on Sunday?" He actually said, "Want to go swimming on Sunday?"

See the difference? I do. Sigh. . . .

SUNDAY, JULY 8

I just don't even know where to start. Maybe at the pool. . . . Alex asked me if I wanted to go swimming today, remember? Sure enough, Alex was there.

It was all cloudy and cool though, so after about an hour we decided (it was Alex's idea) to go somewhere else. It sure seemed like something was bothering him, and I thought, Well, maybe he was sorry he asked me to meet him there, and maybe he was trying to think of a way to get rid of me. We went to this little park near the pool and sat on a picnic table. For a while we just read all the names carved into the table, and I was about to say that I had to go home (just in case he did want to get rid of me, I thought I'd better make it sound like I was ready to go anyway), when he said, "I got the strangest phone message the other day."

"What message?"

"Some girl called and said to my mother, 'Tell Alex I love him.'" Then he looked at me as if he was waiting for me to confess.

Boy was I *mad*. I was mad because, first of all, it wasn't ME who called, but Alex thought it was, and second of all, I was wondering who in the heck DID call. Grrrr. But before I could say anything, Alex looks up because this girl is walking toward us. She's smiling and waving her arm like crazy, and when she gets pretty close, she says, "Hiiiiiii! Hiiiiiii there!"

It was Christy, from school. I thought I was going to have a heart attack.

She started drooling all over Alex. "Hiiiii, Alex. Oh hi, Mary Lou. Whatever are you doing over here, Alex? I'm here with my cousin. Did you ever meet my cousin Carol? She's up there," and she pointed toward the pool and batted her eyelashes at Alex and wiggled her shoulders and SAT DOWN next to Alex on the picnic table.

"Hi," said Alex.

I didn't say one word.

"So, what are you *doing* over here, Alex? Huh? Huh?"

"Nothing."

"*Nothing?* So why are you over *here* doing nothing? You live way over in *Norton!!*" She turned to me and said, "Have you ever seen Alex's house? *I* have. I just *love* your mom, Alex. She's so *sweet.* . . ."

On and on and on she went, babbling away like that, asking about a million questions and never giving Alex a chance to answer anything. I didn't think she was *ever* going to leave. I started counting the leaves on this tree next to the table, just to keep from punching her one. I got up to 367 before she finally said, "So hey, Alex, why don't you come up and go swimming with me and my cousin? Oh, you too, Mary Lou. Come on, Alex, won't you?" Wiggle wiggle. Smile smile.

And then Alex said, "Can't. Have to go home."

So she made this little pouty mouth and said, "Well, Carol's waiting for me. I'll let you off this time, Alex. . . ." Wiggle wiggle. Smile smile. And, at last, she got up and wiggled away.

We sat there for a few minutes. Then I said, "Do you really have to go home now?"

And he said, "Nope."

Then I said, "I think I just figured out who left that phone message."

He looked a little disappointed. "Huh?"

"Well, it wasn't *me*!" And I gave a meaningful look in Christy's direction. She was still wiggling off in the distance.

"Ahhh," he said.

And then you would not believe what he did next.

He put his hand on top of mine. At first I didn't know if it was an accident or on purpose and I was wondering if I should move my hand. But he pressed his down a little bit, so I figured it was on purpose. Then I started wondering if I should turn my hand *over*—then he could hold it—but what if he didn't *want* to hold it? How am I supposed to know what he's *thinking*? I decided to leave my hand the way it was. If he wanted to turn it over, he could do that himself.

When I think about it right now, I could just swoon away.

And then do you know what he said? He said, "I like you, Mary Lou Finney."

And I just sat there like some idiot. I just sat there staring at him. . . .

Anyway, then Alex got up and he said, "I'll walk you home," and he TOOK MY HAND (which turned over automatically, I think) and we walked home, and I still couldn't talk at all, and just before we got to the corner of my street I pretended I had to scratch my ankle so I could let go of his hand because even though I really liked holding his hand, I would have died if anyone in my family saw that. . . .

MONDAY, JULY 9

Mary Lou Cheevey. Mrs. Alex Cheevey. Mary Lou and Alex. Mary Lou Finney and Alex Cheevey.

I can hardly breathe.

I didn't even go out of the house today in case Alex called—which he didn't and I think I will probably die if he doesn't.

Oh, God! What am I saying? I hate it when girls moon over boys. I refuse to moon over Alex Cheevey.

But Lord! All day long I kept coming up to my room and lying on my

i lov

bed so I could remember exactly what happened yesterday and exactly what it felt like holding his hand, and really, if someone else said this to me I would throw up. . . .

WEDNESDAY, JULY 11

Alex had to work all day and couldn't come over, but he did call. . . .

THURSDAY, JULY 12

I think all of a sudden I realize why Beth Ann wouldn't tell me about Derek and why she's soooo strange these days. Because I'm acting just as weird as she is, I swear. I'm turning into a real lunatic. All over a boy. I cannot believe it. I am going to try not to act like this. But I see why Beth Ann didn't want to talk about Derek. You want to keep it floating around in your mind and keep it secret, because there is no way you can explain it to anyone without sounding like a complete idiot.

But I am really going to try. I am going to be reasonable about this. . . . (But God! I LOVE ALEX CHEEVEY!!!!!!)

THURSDAY, JULY 19

I . . . saw Alex again today, but couldn't go anywhere with him because I had to help Maggie take care of Dennis and Dougie. . . .

But Alex and I did get to be alone for about ten whole minutes. Sighhhhh. Here's what happened. We were sitting on the front porch, and he said, "I like it when you wear that pink shirt." (I was wearing a pink T-shirt.) I never thought boys noticed what girls wore. . . . And *then* Alex reached over and touched the sleeve of my shirt, as if he was checking out its pinkness or something. Well, when he touched that sleeve, I thought, Oh boy, this is it, he's going to kiss me now. I could just feel it coming. I was dissolving into a blithering idiot.

But then Tommy started banging on the door behind us, and Alex moved his hand (alas, alas!), and Maggie said I had to go in, and I looked at Alex and he looked at me, and I said, "I like it when you wear that blue shirt" (he was wearing his blue T-shirt), and he smiled.

Ohhhhh. Is this disgusting or what? What's the matter with me? Do you think he was going to kiss me? I wish there was a manual for this sort of thing, something that would tell you about holding hands and kissing. When should this happen? How many days should you hold hands before you kiss? Sometimes I just can't wait for that kiss, but sometimes, I think, *Ugh! Please don't!* I wish I'd make up my mind. I wonder if Alex thinks the same things. Do boys actually think about this mushy stuff? Or do they just automatically know what to do?

WEDNESDAY, JULY 25

Here is something for my manual: When the guy puts his arm around the girl while walking along, the girl might find it more comfortable to also put her arm around him at this time. She can put it sort of across his back. It is a little difficult to walk this way, and you won't want to walk very far like this, but it's a neat thing to do. The girl will find it difficult to think of things to say during this time, but the boy will carry on about something or other (basketball, for example), and the girl can get by with saying, "Mmmm" or "Ah" or "Oh?" This way she can concentrate primarily on not tripping.

When other people do these things, it looks so *easy*. Don't let that fool you. . . .

MONDAY, AUGUST 6

Alex said, "Want to go see my fishing lures?"

The funny thing is Alex really *does* have a collection of fishing lures. We went out into the garage to look at them, and then it happened. The Big Event.

He KISSED me!!!!

Sighhhhhhhh.

Right there in the garage, beside the fishing lures. He just leaned over and kissed me. It was simple as anything. . . .

Sighhhhhhhh.

After the kiss, we looked at some more fishing lures. It was a little embarrassing, if you want to know the truth. I am sure we were both thinking, Wow! We did it! We kissed. Wow! And there we were saying things like, "Oh that's a nice lure," and "Here's my favorite" . . . Then, right before we went back into the house, we kissed one more time. I started that one. I figured maybe it was my turn. Is that how it goes?

Sighhhhhh . . .

sighhh..

YOU COULD BE YOUR OWN WORST ENEMY

by Latoya Hunter

Thursday, June 13, 1996
A little after midnight, alone in my room

Dear Diary,
A few minutes ago the clock struck twelve A.M., and at that very moment I turned eighteen, crossing over the threshold into a new world where I, Latoya Hunter, am legally a woman!!

It's funny, but I just looked in the mirror and saw the same person I saw yesterday. There was not even a hint of new maturity or sophistication dancing in my eyes. I suppose that will come with time, as I explore my new universe.

I often wonder what kind of woman I will become. I dream that I will be one with the poise of Oprah Winfrey, the wisdom and class of Ms. Maya Angelou, the respectability of Colin Powell, and the caring, nurturing ways of Louise Williamson, my grandmother. I believe that then I would simply shine!

People have told me that I already shine in their eyes. They see me and they see someone who has accomplished a great deal in only eighteen years. They say, "Wow! You had a book published at twelve years old! That's amazing!" or "That's really impressive that you started college a year ahead of time." I say, "Thank you," and offer a little smile.

Confession: Sometimes the smiles are forced and fake. How could they all be genuine when there has always been someone telling me that I just wasn't good enough? The person was a beast that has existed inside of me for so long, feeding on my doubts and fears (I guess it's true: We are at times our own worst enemy). Every day I struggled to love myself, to smile at the imperfect image I saw in the mirror, and even to laugh at the clumsiness that is second nature to me. I tried to remember that I am intelligent, and that people say I am polite and kind.

I strived to accept Latoya Hunter, a girl who has her full share of flaws. But at times I wanted to curse the mirror for sending back the reflection of someone I thought would never mesmerize anyone with her beauty or have admiring eyes cast upon her when she walked into a room. I said little or nothing around strangers because I didn't believe that I could provoke laughter or that I had enough wit to make a decent contribution to a conversation. I shied away from my word processor because I feared failing at writing, the thing I love best.

Now here I am. I am eighteen years old and longing to blossom into a "phenomenal woman," as Maya would put it.

Pretty women wonder where my secret lies.
I'm not cute or built to suit a fashion model's size
But when I start to tell them,
They think I'm telling lies.
I say,
It's in the reach of my arms,
The span of my hips,
The stride of my step,
The curl of my lips.
I'm a woman
Phenomenally.
Phenomenal woman,
That's me.

That's all of the poem I've memorized so far.

Deep inside I know that I will never truly be phenomenal if the beast continues to live within me. That's why today I will murder the monster with the only weapon that could ever do the job—self-love. There is nothing more powerful. It cannot fail me.

So on this morning of June 13, 1996, I want to declare that I am beautiful, I am charming, I am intelligent, I am talented, and as long as I believe it, Latoya Hunter will go places! It's in the glimmer of my mind's eye, the smoothness of my voice, the shine of my hair, the depth of my thinking.

Now if only I can *keep this up* when I leave my room.

17

IT'S OKAY

by Joan Jacobs Brumberg

I like to have an occasional conversation with myself. Although I'm an adult, a professor of history, and a grandmother, I still need to talk to myself to find out what I really feel and think. That's why I keep a diary.

Writing in a diary is such a helpful thing to do, especially when you're a teenager facing new emotions, problems, and opportunities. It's definitely the best place for saying things you've always wanted to say but think you shouldn't. Unlike your mother, your sister, or your best friend, a diary doesn't get hurt, angry, or hold grudges.

A diary lets you move at your own pace. It doesn't push you to get the

to talk to yourself

words out quickly (the way you need to in an argument), and it doesn't shush you up when you're really on a roll. In a diary there are no assigned topics the way there are in school, and no one checks your spelling or punctuation—unless *you* want to. A diary is a safe haven, a place to talk to yourself about what (or who) you think is important, wonderful, confusing, or infuriating.

Because diaries are such reliable listeners, American girls have been talking to them for nearly two hundred years. In the early 1800s, after the American Revolution, when public schools began to include girls as well as boys, girls began to discover the pleasures of writing as well as reading. By the time of the Civil War, many girls were taking up pen and ink to write their own stories and poems, and also to keep diaries.

Young women in the past lived very different lives from the lives girls live today, but their diaries tell us what issues were closest to their hearts. Long ago, when the activities of most families and communities centered around the church, girls talked to their diaries mostly about their faith in God and asked for spiritual guidance in the effort to be good. Social events, clothes, and shopping were rarely mentioned.

By 1900 more and more girls were attending high school, and their diaries began to sound more familiar to us. These diarists reported on school activities, worried about girlfriends and hairstyles, and dropped shy hints about their special interest in "the opposite sex." At this point in time girls' diaries—like their lives—were still controlled by powerful ideas about what women and girls should and should not talk about.

Today teenage girls talk to their diaries with much greater honesty about all kinds of subjects. No topic seems too silly or too serious. Some diarists have complaints about family members, teachers, even the President. Others describe feelings stimulated by a particular book, movie, or film star. Many write repeatedly about their special relationships with close friends or a particular boy. I've read detailed accounts of lengthy phone calls as well as graphic details of passionate kisses. I've also listened to diarists who feel misunderstood and badly treated, and to many who dislike themselves because they think they are ugly or dumb.

I'm able to describe the "inside" of girls' diaries because I've read almost two hundred of them written between 1830 and 1990. Many of the older historic diaries I've read are found in libraries and historical societies in small towns as well as big cities across the United States. The newer ones were generally loaned to me by people who understood my desire to learn more about "girl history," a very important part of women's history.

Treasure your diary, for the things you write in it now will have meaning beyond your teenage years—both to you and to people like me, who study the lives of women and girls in the past, who watch the way in which generations of American girls have used diaries as they pass through adolescence into adulthood.

When, as a woman, you revisit your girlhood diary, it will not only be a lot of fun because of all the memories it will provoke, but it will also be a way to take your own measure, to see the distance you have traveled since you were a girl. If you one day happen to have a daughter or a granddaughter, your diary will provide both of you with a way to talk about how girls' lives have changed or how they have stayed the same.

You need not be an Anne Frank or the daughter of famous or wealthy people to have a diary that is important to history. In fact, the diaries I find most interesting are those written by ordinary girls. So as you write, remember that American girls have always enjoyed this particular form of self-expression and that girlhood diaries will probably never be "extinct" because of our need to talk to ourselves about ourselves in this very important way.

18

EVERYONE'S A LITTLE

STRANGE

by Rebecca Goldstein

The wind was a torrent of darkness among the gusty trees,
The moon was a ghostly galleon tossed upon cloudy seas.
The road was a ribbon of moonlight over the purple moor,
And the highwayman came riding—
Riding—riding—

And the voices kept on droning—droning—droning—

The highwayman came riding, up to the old inn-door.

She had the worst seat in the class. It was right up front, isolated from everyone else, with Mrs. Crowl looming up over her like some sort of evil bird of prey. With those little beady eyes hovering over her head, it wasn't even possible for Samantha to doodle, much less read under her desk. Death by boredom was a distinct possibility, especially on days like this, when she had to suffer through a double period of English.

How many more stunningly obvious questions could Mrs. Crowl claw out of that poem? "The Highwayman" was a long poem. It was a very long poem. Good old Alfred Noyes hadn't believed in taking any shortcuts. And boy had he liked metaphors. He was like a metaphor maniac. "The Highwayman" was an English teacher's dream. "What is a galleon? . . . What do you think he meant by 'ghostly galleon'? . . . Why would the poet say 'galleon' rather than 'merchant ship'?"

Like maybe because he was a poet, Mrs. Crowl.

Samantha glanced around at the rest of the class. She couldn't believe how many of the kids were actually raising their hands, bothering to answer Mrs. Crowl's astoundingly stupid questions.

Mrs. Crowl had given Samantha this honored seat out of some sort of lowdown teacher spite. This was the first English teacher she'd ever had who didn't like her. She had been used to having English teachers gushingly read her assignments aloud to the class. It was already late April, and Mrs. Crowl had never once come close to gushing. Instead Samantha's essays came back to her with spiteful-looking B's scrawled in red across them, sometimes even B minuses. The comments were things like, "This is well written, but you did not address the question asked," or more often, there was just a snarling "Unclear."

"Unclear to a moron," Samantha silently snarled back.

And the highwayman came riding—
Riding—riding—

Her best friend Judy had a really great seat for English. Not only was it in the last row, up against the back wall, but it was between two really hot guys. The hottest of the two by far was Pete. Pete had this longish hair, dark blond, that the school periodically hassled him about. Their school had a pretty strict dress code that Pete took special pride in flouting. The boys were supposed to wear ties, and once Pete, smiling wickedly, had come in with a pale green bow tie. Of all Pete's smiles, Samantha loved his wicked one the best.

And he rode with a jeweled twinkle,
His pistol butts a-twinkle,
His rapier hilt a-twinkle, under the jeweled sky.

Judy had confessed to Samantha last weekend that she really liked Pete, but Samantha hadn't confessed back. It would have been too stupid, a mutual confessing fest. And anyway, if she had ever been at all tempted to confess, she would have done it ages ago. She had liked Pete since way, way long ago, since last year, the very beginning of seventh grade. Judy, on the other hand, had only just gotten around to categorizing Pete as hot. Before too long, Samantha knew, Judy'd be confessing to her about some other guy.

Any chance Samantha got to turn around, she'd turn, always to see Judy and Pete whispering together. She knew Judy well enough to know what that look in Judy's dark eyes meant. After all, they had been best friends since second grade.

Back in the second grade, Judy had been a new kid in the school. She had moved here from Massachusetts, all alone with her mother. She was an only child, and her father had died.

When Judy moved in, she had a long dark braid, so long she could sit on it. Samantha had been fascinated by that long hair. Her own mother made her keep her blond hair short, since long hair was too much trouble. When she'd pointed out Judy's hair, her mother had responded that Judy's mother no doubt had all the time in the world, having only one daughter to look after. Samantha's mother had three daughters, one son, and not enough help.

Judy had been a little bit overweight back then, too—not really fat, just pudgy enough to make gym a daily misery. That had been an immediate bond between the two of them, their dislike of gym, their dread of the ordeal of team picking.

Samantha could still remember that she had been a little nervous about going over to Judy's house for the first time. She had thought it would be a really sad place, with only Judy and her mother living there. Every time she had thought about living all alone with only a mother, she'd felt sorry for Judy. Of course, that had been before she had met Terry, Judy's mother.

Terry, who had told Samantha right away to call her by her first name, had long dark hair, too, though not as long as Judy's, and big dark shining eyes. She didn't look like any other mother. One of the things Terry loved to do with them, even back then when they were little kids, was dance. She loved rock 'n' roll and had taught Samantha how to really shake it.

At first, when Samantha had started going over there, she had found Terry so odd for a mother that she had thought it was almost as if Judy didn't have a father *or* a mother. Maybe Terry was like a friend, but she sure wasn't like

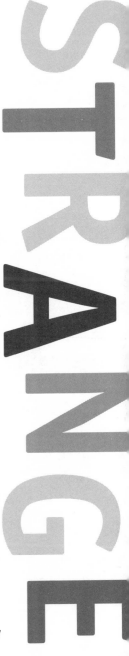

a mother. It had seemed to Samantha that *real* mothers (like her own) didn't even like Terry. But then Samantha had gotten used to Terry. It had turned out to be pretty easy to get used to Terry. By now it took a really concentrated effort to remember ever having felt sorry for Judy.

> Over the cobbles he clattered and clashed in the dark inn-
> yard.
> He tapped with his whip on the shutters, but all was locked
> and barred.
> He whistled a tune to the window, and who should be waiting
> there
> But the landlord's black-eyed daughter,
> Bess, the landlord's daughter,
> Plaiting a dark red love-knot into her long black hair.

Between sixth and seventh grade Judy had gone from being pudgy to being gorgeous, just like her mother. She had cut off her long braid, so that her thick dark hair fell just past her shoulders. People sometimes mistook Judy and Terry for sisters, which they both thought was hilarious. And now there were boys taking lots of notice of Judy. Boys like Pete.

> And dark in the dark old inn-yard a stable-wicket creaked
> Where Tim the ostler listened. His face was white and
> peaked.
> His eyes were hollows of madness...

"Who can tell me what an ostler is?"

Samantha knew. She knew all sorts of arcane words—like, for example, "arcane"—because she was always reading, and her favorite books were big, sprawling nineteenth-century novels, chock-full of arcane words. But of course she would never deign to answer a question of Mrs. Crowl's, not even when it was a question that she was pretty certain nobody else could answer. She had given up answering any questions of Mrs. Crowl's with that very first B minus that had come back on the first essay she'd written. Samantha had stared at that B minus in disbelief. The assignment had been to write on a favorite poem, and Samantha had written on Edgar Allan Poe's "The Raven." "I don't understand what you're trying to say" had been Mrs. Crowl's response.

She was only a little surprised now when Mrs. Crowl called on Pete. One of Samantha's secret theories about Pete was that he was almost as fond of reading as she was, though of course he took greater pains to hide it. But every once in a while he said something that almost betrayed him.

"Doesn't it mean like someone who takes care of horses, like sort of a stable hand?"

"Excellent, Peter. That's exactly what 'ostler' means. It was used especially for someone who took care of the horses at an inn."

Samantha took advantage of the excuse for turning around that Pete's speaking gave her. There was Judy, her cheek resting on her open palm, her face slightly toward him as he spoke. He glanced over at Judy and shrugged a little, as if telling her that his answer had only been a lucky guess.

"Now what do you think the poet means by 'hollows of madness'? What could the poet have meant by calling Tim's eyes 'hollows of madness'?"

Samantha had known it was coming. A metaphor like "hollows of madness" would not get by unprobed by Mrs. Crowl. Soon Mrs. Crowl was going to be asking something like: Why do you think the poet said "hollows of madness" instead of "crannies of craziness" or "potholes of psychosis"?

She turned around to look at the clock on the side wall, after first betting against herself on how many minutes had elapsed since her last time check. She lost bad. Only seven minutes had gone by. It was amazing how much *time* seven minutes could take up. There were still eighteen minutes of double English left to go. At least it was the last period of the day before homeroom.

The discussion was still droning on and on about poor old Tim's hollows of madness. How could they not see it when it was so pathetically obvious? How much longer could this thing drag itself out? It was getting indecent. Before she even knew what she was doing, her hand shot up into the air.

"Yes, Samantha." Mrs. Crowl pointed her bony face down at her. Her resemblance to some sort of killer Alfred Hitchcock bird was uncanny.

"Tim had mad eyes because he was completely and madly in love, and he was completely and insanely jealous. It's like he'd been hollowed out, with nothing else left in him, with only his hopeless love and jealousy staring out."

There was a moment of absolute silence, and then the entire class burst out laughing. Even Mrs. Crowl cracked her beak and laughed, which had to be some sort of major violation of teacher rules.

"No, Samantha," Mrs. Crowl said, her thin lips curling into a smile that looked downright nasty. "I don't think we have to go to such lengths to explain what the poet meant by 'hollows of madness.' I think he was merely telling us that Tim the ostler was crazy."

Normally Samantha would have just racked up the comment to Mrs. Crowl's excessive idiocy. But that was hardly possible now, with the whole class laughing over what she'd just said. She wished that there was some unobvious way for her to turn around and see whether Pete and Judy were laughing. She could just imagine it, Judy's dark eyes flashing up into Pete's green eyes. In fact, for the rest of the period Samantha could imagine nothing else.

She would have been very happy never to have heard another reference to "The Highwayman" for as long as she lived. But later that day as she walked home with Judy, just as they did almost every day after school, her best friend said, "Do you know what Pete said to me when you said that thing about the poem in Mrs. Crowl's class? He said that it was just the kind of thing you *would* say."

Samantha said nothing. She was almost at the point of asking Judy whether she agreed with Pete, but then she didn't, afraid that Judy would say yes.

After leaving Judy off at her house, Samantha walked the rest of the six blocks to her house with Pete's words playing again and again in her head. She could just picture him saying it and Judy leaning her head into her open palm and listening with a little smile. Judy had been smiling just now when she'd repeated Pete's words to her.

"He said it was just the kind of thing you *would* say."

Maybe it's me, she suddenly thought now. Maybe I'm the strange one. Of course, she hadn't seemed strange to herself. But then strange people never do.

"He said it was just the kind of thing you *would* say."

If Pete was saying that, then not only must it be obvious to everyone else that she was strange, but even worse, there must be some sort of recognizable *pattern* to her strangeness. She was suddenly almost grateful for the B minuses that had made her angry enough to shut up in class. Think how many times she might have made a fool of herself! Maybe from now on she'd be much better off if instead of speaking, she just listened silently to everyone else, the ones who weren't strange, the ones who said what everyone else was thinking. She would try to think just like they did. And until she knew exactly how they did it, she'd just try to keep quiet. She'd work on herself, work really hard, until there was nothing at all strange left to her.

"Strange." The word, suddenly seeming sharp-edged and dangerous, went ricocheting around in her head, doing damage. "She's so strange," she thought, only hearing the sentence said in her mother's voice.

Samantha had often, in fact, heard her mother saying exactly that, especially when Samantha had been little and had first become friends with Judy.

"I feel sorry for that little girl," Samantha's mother used to say. "With no father and that strange woman for a mother."

Sometimes her mother still let loose a condescending "strange" about Terry. So Terry, too, was strange, at least from the point of view of Samantha's mother. In fact, now that Samantha thought about it, Terry was probably strange from the point of view of a good many other people besides Samantha's mother. Even Samantha herself, when she had been too young to know any better, had felt that there was something wrong about Terry just because there was something so right about her.

"Strange," she said now out loud. And slowly, very slowly, Samantha began to smile.

19

Looking In Is
Looking Out
Is Looking In

by Jeanne Moutoussamy-Ashe

Once you accept your
uniqueness and see it as
something special, you can
respect the differences
in others. A deep love
of self empowers you to
excel and gives you
the ability to focus on the
needs of others.

preju

by M. E. Kerr

"It was Christmas," said my grandmother, "and I went from the boarding school in Switzerland with my roommate, to her home in Germany.

"She was afraid it would not be grand enough for me there . . . that because my family lived in New York, it would seem too modest, and she kept saying, 'We live very simply,' and she kept saying, 'Except for my uncle Karl, who pays my tuition, we are not that rich.'

"I told her no, no, this is thrilling to me, and I meant it. Everywhere there was Christmas: wreaths of *Tannenbaum* hung, the Christmas markets were still open in the little towns we passed through. Every house had its *Christbaum*—a tall evergreen with a star on top.

"I was not then a religious Jew. I was a child from a family that did not believe in religion . . . and what I felt was envy, and joy at the activity: the Christmas-card landscape, snow falling, smoke rising from chimneys, and villagers rushing through the streets with gift-wrapped packages, and the music of Christmas.

"Then we saw the signs outside her village.

"*Juden unerwünscht.* (Jews not welcome.)

"And other, smaller signs, saying things in German like kinky hair and hooked noses not wanted here, and worse, some so vile I can't say them to you.

"'These have nothing to do with us,' Inge said. 'These are just political, to do with this new chancellor, Hitler. Pay no attention, Ruth.'

dice isn't pretty

"I did not really even think of myself as a Jew, and while I was shocked, I did not take it personally since I was from America. We even had our own Christmas tree when I was a tiny child. . . . Now I was *your* age, Alison. Sixteen.

"Her parents rushed out to greet us, and welcome us. Inside there was candlelight and mistletoe and wonderful smells of food cooking, and we were hungry after the long trip. The house was filled with the family, the little children dressed up, everyone dressed up and joyous.

"We sat around a huge table, and wine was served to the adults, and Inge's mother said we girls could have half a glass ourselves. We felt grown-up. We sipped the wine and Christmas carols played over the radio, but there was so much talk, it was like a thin sound of the season with in front of us the tablecloth, best china, crystal glasses! I thought, What does she mean she lives modestly? There were servants . . . and it looked like a little house from the outside only. Inside it was big and lively, with presents under the tree we would open later. I was so impressed and delighted to be included.

"Then a maid appeared and in a sharp voice said, 'Frau Kantor? There is something I must say.'

"Inge's mother looked annoyed. 'What *is* it?'

"Then this thin woman in her crisp white uniform with the black apron said, 'I cannot serve the food. I do not hand food to a man, woman, or child'—her eyes on me suddenly—'of Jewish blood ever again.'"

My grandmother paused and shook her head.

I said, "What happened then?"

"Then," my grandmother said, "we carried our plates into the kitchen and served ourselves . . . All except for Inge's uncle Karl, who left because he had not known until that moment that I was Inge's *Jewish* friend from her school."

"I never heard that you were there when all of that was going on, Grandma."

"It was my one and only time in Germany," she said. "So you don't have to tell me about what it feels like to be an outsider. You don't have to tell me about prejudice. But Alison, I thank you for telling me about yourself. I'm proud that you told me first."

A week later, my mother said, "Why do you have to *announce* it, Alison?"

"Is that all you're going to say?"

"No, that's first. First I'm going to say there was no need to announce it. You think I don't know what's going on with you and Laura? I don't need eyes in the back of my head to figure that out."

"But it makes you uncomfortable to *hear* it from me, is that it?"

"I can't do anything about it, can I? I see it every time you bring her here. I would like to believe it's a stage you're going through, but from what I've read and heard, it isn't."

"No. It isn't."

"I can kiss grandchildren good-bye, I guess, if you persist with this choice."

"Mom, it's not a choice. Was it a choice when you fell in love with Dad?"

"Most definitely. I chose him!"

"What I mean is—you didn't choose him over a woman."

"I would never choose a woman, Alison! Never! Life is family. Or I *used* to think it was. Before *this*!"

"What I mean is—there were only males you were attracted to."

"Absolutely! Where you got this—it wasn't from *me*."

"So what if the world was different, and men loved men and women loved women, but you were still *you*? What would you do?"

My mother shrugged. "Find another world, I guess."

"So that's what *I* did. I found another world."

"Good! Fine! You have your world and I have mine. Mine happens to be the *real* world, but never mind. You always went your own way."

Then she sighed and said, "I'm only glad your father's not alive to hear his favorite daughter tell him she's *gay*."

"I was his *only* daughter, Mother."

"All the more reason . . . We dreamed of the day you'd bring our grand-children to us."

"That's still an option. I may bring a grandchild to you one day."

"Don't."

"Don't?"

"Not if it's one of those test-tube/artificial-insemination children. I'm talking about a real child, a child of our blood, with a mother *and* a father. I don't care to have one of those kids I see on Donahue who was made with a turkey baster or some other damn thing! Alison, what you've gotten your-self involved in is not just a matter of me saying, Oh, so you're *gay,* fine, and then life goes on. What you've gotten yourself involved in is *serious*!"

"That's why I'm telling you about it."

"That's not why you're telling me about it!"

"Why am I telling you about it?"

"You want me to say it's okay with me. You gays want the whole world to say it's okay to be gay!"

"And it isn't."

"No, it is *not*! Okay? I've said how I feel! You are what you are, okay, but it is not okay with me what you are!"

"So where do we go from here?"

"I'll tell you where not to go! Don't go to the neighbors, and don't go to my friends, and don't go to your grandmother!"

"What do you think Grandmother would say?"

"When she stopped weeping?"

"You think she'd weep?"

"Alison," my mother said, "it would *kill* your grandmother!"

"You think Grandma wouldn't understand?"

"I *know* Grandmother wouldn't understand! What is to understand? She has this grandchild who'll never bring her great-grandchildren."

"I might bring her some straight from the Donahue show."

"Very funny. *Very* funny," my mother said. Then she said, "Alison, this coming-out thing isn't working. You came out to me, all right, I'm your mother and maybe you had to come out to me. But where your grandmother's concerned: Keep quiet."

"You think she'd want that?"

"I think she doesn't even *dream* such a thing could come up! She's had enough *tsuris* in life. Back in the old country there were relatives lost in the Holocaust! Isn't that enough for one woman to suffer in a lifetime?"

"Maybe that would make her more sympathetic."

"Don't compare gays with Jews—there's no comparison."

"I'm both. There's prejudice against both. And I didn't choose to be either."

"If you want to kill an old woman before her time, tell her."

"I think you have Grandmother all wrong."

"If I have Grandmother all wrong," said my mother, "then I don't know her and you don't know me, and we might as well all be strangers."

"To be continued," I wrote in my diary that night.

My grandmother knew . . . my mother knew . . . one day my mother would know that my grandmother knew.

All coming-out stories are a continuing process.

Strangers take a long time to become acquainted, particularly when they are from the same family.

21

Popularity Peaks

by Tabitha Soren
with additional reporting by Julie Cooper

All names have been changed.

You could surf Jodi Burda's feathered mane, it was so perfectly coiffed. Not only was she Miss Freshman, class president, cheerleading captain, prom queen, and recipient of the teachers'-pet-driven Special Student award, but Jodi also had the cutest boyfriend, the biggest bra, the best grades, the coolest clothes, and parents who would seemingly buy her anything. On top of it, she had ten friends just like her.

Katrina Kramer, on the other hand, was stringbean skinny, splattered with freckles, and had feet the size of canoes. Instead of her parents taking her to the mall to buy her the latest velour sweater and add-a-bead neck-

lace that all the popular kids were wearing, her wardrobe consisted mostly of clothes her mother made. She battled with her parents almost daily over her right to wear the makeup that every other girl at her school was allowed to wear. She was sure that her plain face was why she didn't fit in and why none of the boys paid any attention to her. And this was only in junior high.

Having grown up in a military family, Katrina was perpetually the new-kid-in-the-class. It was impossible for her to ever feel completely accepted because she hadn't known so-and-so "since kindergarten." In school after school she worked double time trying to fit in. In junior high she tried out in front of the entire school for the cheerleading squad. Twice she endured the agony of wondering if they would think she was cool enough, pretty enough, and popular enough to actually make the squad. Cheerleading skills had little to do with it. One time she made it and one time she didn't.

Every morning she'd spend an hour curling her hair, hoping to get it to look like Jodi Burda's. She went to the parties of the popular kids whenever they asked and didn't get mad when they boycotted hers. But no matter what she did, her popularity rating never soared. Instead of being the glamorous Jodi Burda, she was just the average Katrina Kramer.

If only Katrina had known that Jodi and her gang were peaking in junior high and that for her, the best was yet to come.

Years later, home on her Christmas break from graduate school, Katrina made her usual trip to the local suburban mall. It was the mall in which she bought her first bra, the mall in which she snuck into her first R-rated movie, the mall in which she got her ears pierced for the first time, the mall in which she had for years desperately tried to make herself into a mini–Jodi Burda.

On this particular Christmas shopping excursion she stopped by the Lancôme counter at Nordstrom's. "As usual, I spotted someone I had gone to junior high and high school with," laughs Katrina. "Here was the prettiest, most popular girl in my graduating class. Senior year she was voted both Most Popular and Most Likely to Be the Next Oprah Winfrey. Before me stood Jodi Burda. Here she was at a cosmetics counter—*behind* a cosmetics counter—in a gray and pink smock looking over the glass counter at me. I was infinitely more hopeful about the fairness of life."

The fact that Jodi Burda ended up selling cosmetics at a mall is not that unusual. Not that there's anything wrong with it, either. But considering the potential Jodi had shown, she could be marketing or manufacturing cosmetics.

Jodi was a victim of peaking.

"I wish it wouldn't have taken me so long to figure out that sometimes the teenager who is having a consistently good time is peaking," says Katrina. "Those seemingly happy

Jodi was a victim of peaking.

teens are the ones who should be really depressed because if you peak in junior high and high school, the only place to go is down."

This sometimes happens because winning the popularity contest so early breeds laziness and an expectation that the rest of the game of life will be as easy as school.

It was my experience that the kids who were popular were also the teachers' pets. In some cases that meant those kids were the best students, but just as many had merely learned the art of sucking up. The latter no doubt grew up to be master networkers, using their charm to rise to middle management positions in conventional companies like IBM. But those teachers' pets might never learn the progressive skills necessary to end up running the company or take the risks to start their own business.

Certainly not every popular kid is doomed. To be fair, some popular teens are popular for a reason. Some of the smartest people I know today were popular in school. They got a lot of attention because they were bright and everyone was always trying to cheat off their papers. The ones who were exceedingly popular were smart *and* nice—they'd let you cheat off them.

Conversely, some of the social misfits who were unpopular in school deserved to be. They were wild risk-takers because they had nothing to lose. They were antisocial to the point of being mean and shared nothing of themselves with other kids. Many of them still haven't learned enough social skills to contribute to the world around them in a meaningful way.

But if you aren't the world's most successful teen, the peaking phenomenon is a good thing to keep in mind. It might take the edge off not having a date to the homecoming game and soothe you when you get another prominent zit on your nose. Ultimately you may just be rewarded for swimming outside the mainstream, because you'll be forced to develop your own style. That makes "Katrinas" more special than merely popular. Knowing that you could end up setting trends for the popular types should take away some of the pain and

Ultimately you may just be rewarded for swimming outside the mainstream.

alienation of living left of center.

It's not a coincidence that so many nerds, outsiders, and freaks end up being very successful later on in life—when it really matters. In the grand scheme of things, junior high and high school don't last that many years. When you're strange, it can make you stronger. Not fitting in forces you to create your own world. If no one likes you, you have a lot of time to run around in your own head, where there's a lot of creativity and freedom. You think Mariah Carey, Bill Gates, Quentin Tarantino, or Dennis Rodman, were popular in high school? Get real.

What these celebrities know and what Katrina eventually found out was that being the last girl asked to the prom, the last kid picked for the PE softball team, or feeling like the only teenager who has no plans on a Friday night, you end up learning to think for yourself and caring less about what other people think—eventually. The process of self-acceptance takes time. But once you reach that state, your eccentricity blossoms in more creative ways, and you become sensitive to emotions and the world around

you in a way that can only happen when life is hard on you and introduces you to sadness and compassion.

There are no surveys to prove the widespread connection between lonerville and success. But just look around you. The school outcasts are usually some of the smartest and most creative people in the building. That group of band geeks, science freaks, and spiky-haired outcasts are independent filmmakers, musicians, and clothing designers of the future. The ones who take a different path often end up being the innovators of society.

Instead of feeling anxious, you might just think about peaking. Why would you want to have it all so early in life? Wouldn't you prefer a life that builds at a nice steady pace? Knowing about peaking could allow you to survive junior high and high school only slightly wounded, suddenly finding yourself in college bonding with the other cool original thinkers, and slowly make a fulfilling career path and realize what great experiences will await you as you keep outpeaking yourself.

> *When you're strange, it can make you stronger.*

GET A GAME PLAN!

by Rebecca Lobo

1. DREAM!!! . . . THEY COME TRUE!

One thing I've realized over the past few years is that everyone should have dreams in her life, which she works at to make come true. Winning an NCAA National Championship and an Olympic gold medal were things I dreamed about as a little girl. I worked toward my dreams, had a lot of help along the way from family and coaches, and now my dreams have been realized.

2. TREAT OTHERS THE WAY YOU WANT TO BE TREATED!

Whenever I come into contact with someone, I try to be nice, polite, and cordial, because I know I don't like it when people are rude or cruel to me. Sometimes when I'm having a rough day, I'm tempted to take it out on other people. I keep from giving in to this negative urge by reminding myself that everyone has feelings and wants to be treated with respect, and that people generally will be nice to me if I am nice to them.

3. SURROUND YOURSELF WITH POSITIVE PEOPLE!

It's easy to be influenced by the people around you. So make it a point to be around those with positive energy—people who want what's best for you, people who understand your goals and priorities. Remember, anyone who tries to lead you down a wrong path, a path you don't want to travel, really is not a friend.

4. DO THE RIGHT THING!

There are a lot of temptations in the world. We make many choices every day, some of which are very difficult. When making a decision, you must feel good about yourself and confident that you are doing the right thing. If you don't feel comfortable making a certain decision, if your gut tells you something isn't right, then it probably isn't.

5. STAND UP FOR WHAT YOU BELIEVE!

Once you know what is right and wrong, you must stand up for your beliefs. When someone is doing the wrong thing, it is time to speak out. This world needs more people with the courage to act on their beliefs. Don't be afraid to speak against injustice. Even if you are picked on for taking a stand and for having high ideals, you must persevere.

6. BE THE BEST YOU CAN BE!

No matter what you do, you should do it to the best of your ability. You should set goals and work as hard as you can to reach these goals. I measure success by how much effort I have put forth, not by other people's assessment of my accomplishments. If I have tried as hard as I can, then I am a success no matter what the result of my endeavor. *Just don't be afraid to try!*

7. SMILE!

Don't be afraid to show when you are happy. Everyone likes being around a person who has a smile on her face. And a smile is infectious. It is hard to be in a bad mood or feel sorry for yourself when you are smiling. There is a lot in this world worth smiling about. Never forget it!

8. HAVE FAITH!

Know in your heart that no matter what, someone always loves you! Also know that someone is always there to forgive you when you do something wrong, as long as you are truly sorry. For me that is God. I feel that no matter what, I have someone looking out for me and protecting me. This has removed a lot of fear from my life.

9. CHALLENGE YOURSELF!

No matter what you do, you need to challenge yourself. People often take the easy way because it involves less work. The only way to become better at anything is by accepting challenges and trying to conquer them. You become a stronger and better person when you are forced to work hard to get something. In addition, the reward seems even sweeter when you've worked extremely hard to reach your goal!

10. BE POSITIVE!

There are a lot of setbacks in life, but with each one you must look for the silver lining. When failure occurs, learn from it. When something does not turn out the way you wanted, take what you've learned to help you succeed the next time. Our basketball team lost plenty of games during my first three years in college. With each loss we learned something that helped us in our next game, and we stayed positive. We went undefeated, 35–0, my senior year!

get
involved!

by Elizabeth Jenkins-Sahlin

Imagine being a married woman in the year 1848. Very likely, nothing you had would be really your own. Any property or money you inherited from your family, and even your personal belongings, would be under your husband's control (and even if you worked, he'd own your wages, too!). Marriage back then also meant you lost your last name and took your husband's.

Things wouldn't have been much better for you if you were a single woman. More than likely, your father or brother or some other male relative would have control over your property. Married or not, most women had little to say about their rights one hundred fifty years ago.

If you were a girl back then, you didn't have many options to look forward to when it came to things like education and career. Few colleges admitted women. Other than schoolteacher, factory worker, and domestic servant, there weren't very many job opportunities open to women.

By the time I was born in 1984, things had changed a whole lot. That is thanks to the many women who devoted their lives to getting women's rights, among them Elizabeth Cady Stanton, my great-great-great-grandmother.

In 1848 she, along with Lucretia Mott, organized, in Seneca Falls, New York, the first women's rights convention.

I'm so proud of the difference she made in the world.

the declaration of sentiments

Seneca Falls: July 19, 1848

We hold these truths to be self-evident: that all men and women are created equal . . .

Resolved, That all laws which prevent woman from occupying such a station in society as her conscience shall dictate, or which place her in a position inferior to that of man, are contrary to the great precept of nature, and therefore of no force or authority.

Resolved, That woman is man's equal—was intended to be so by the Creator, and the highest good of the race demands that she should be recognized as such. . . .

Resolved, That woman has too long rested satisfied in the circumscribed limits which corrupt customs and a perverted application of the Scriptures have marked out for her, and that it is time she should move in the enlarged sphere which her great Creator has assigned her.

Resolved, That it is the duty of the women of this country to secure to themselves their sacred right to the elective franchise. . . .

Elizabeth Cady Stanton was born in 1815 and grew up in Johnstown, New York. Her father, Daniel Cady, was a lawyer who eventually became an associate justice of the New York State Supreme Court. I've been told that the only person who was not in awe of him was his wife, Margaret, the granddaughter of a Revolutionary War veteran. One historian has summed up Elizabeth Cady Stanton's mother as "strong-minded and self-reliant."

There is a story about Elizabeth Cady Stanton that shows us she, too, was strong-minded very early on. When she was about nine years old, Lizzie, as she was called, overheard her father, Judge Cady, talking to a woman about a problem she had. He read her laws from his law books.

BACK: Elizabeth Cady Stanton, flanked by Nora Stanton Barney and Harriot Stanton Blatch.

FRONT: Elizabeth Jenkins-Sahlin, flanked by her grandma Rhoda and her mom, Coline.

Yes, her husband, who was a drunk, had every right to take the wages she earned. Lizzie hated hearing that. So one day she planned to sneak into his office with scissors in hand and cut out the pages of the law books. When her father discovered her plan, he asked her why she was going to do that. Lizzie answered that she didn't like the laws because they were unfair. She thought that if she got rid of the pages in her father's law books that denied women rights, she would get rid of the law. Daniel Cady pointed out to his daughter that there were more law books, and more important, cutting up law books wouldn't make a difference. "If you don't like the laws, Lizzie," he said, "you have to change them."

When Lizzie became a woman, she worked hard to do just that.

Elizabeth Cady Stanton worked her whole life trying to get people to understand that "all men *and* women are created equal." With the help of Susan B. Anthony, Sojourner Truth, Lucy Stone, Lucretia Mott, and many others, she changed history by convincing the government to let women vote. Once women got to vote nationwide in 1920, they had a say in what laws were to be made.

Elizabeth Cady Stanton passed on her spirit to her seven kids. Her daughter Harriot Stanton Blatch, my great-great-grandmother, was the one to follow most closely in her footsteps. She worked with her mother and Susan B. Anthony on *History of Woman Suffrage,* the first three volumes of which were published in the 1880s. After she married an Englishman, she became active in England's suffragette movement. (Englishwomen couldn't vote either.) When Harriot moved back to the United States in the 1900s, she organized big parades in New York City. Thousands of women and men watched marchers go by, carrying banners that read WORKING WOMEN NEED VOTES TO END BAD WORKING CONDITIONS and VOTES FOR WOMEN!

These are just some of the things that Harriot Stanton Blatch did that helped pass the Nineteenth Amendment to the Constitution, which gave women the right to vote. Unfortunately, Elizabeth Cady Stanton did not live to see this day. She died in 1902, eighteen years before women got the vote.

Harriot Stanton Blatch had two kids—Helen, who died very young, and my great-grandmother, Nora Stanton Barney, who was a civil engineer. In her time, a woman engineer was practically unheard of. As a matter of fact, she was one of the first women in the United States, if not the world, to become a civil engineer. My great-grandmother was also a very talented architect, and most of the houses she designed are located in Greenwich, Connecticut, where I live.

My great-grandma Nora passed on a good bit of property to the next generation—to her three kids, one of whom is Rhoda Barney Jenkins, my grandma, who, just like her mother, became an architect. (She even designed the house I currently live in!)

Caring, loving, fair. These words all describe Grandma Rhoda, who frequently supports organizations that she thinks will help make the world a better place. One of them is Nuclear Freeze, a group trying to keep nuclear weapons from being made. Rhoda is also an active member of the National Organization for Women, which helps change laws that are unfair to women and children. My grandma has received the Eleanor Roosevelt Award from the Connecticut Chapter of NOW, and from the Greenwich Chapter she got a plaque that said RHODA JENKINS: LEADER, ORGANIZER, RABBLE-ROUSER, INSPIRATION. FOR THIS WE THANK YOU.

Grandma Rhoda had two kids—a boy named Morgan and a girl named Coline, who grew up to be my mom, Coline Jenkins-Sahlin.

In 1989, when my mother ran for elected office in Greenwich, Connecticut, she made me her "campaign manager." Even though I was only four years old then, I drove around with my mom, helping her distribute campaign fliers. Mom won the election and is now an official in the legislative body, which passes laws and budgets for the town. She is one of many thousands of women today who do something about laws that affect women as well as men. Most important, she loves me and my brother very much and makes sure we get a very good education. She wants us to become the very best that we can be.

I am very lucky. I have a lot of options to look forward to. I will be allowed to vote when I turn eighteen. I will also have the opportunity to choose any career I want in life. I have thought about what jobs I am interested in, and my favorite ones are musician/singer, writer, and architect. I love skating, but I doubt I'd ever be good enough to be a professional because I have so many other priorities, so I guess that's just one of my dreams.

One of my family's dreams for a long, long time was that the woman suffrage statue would one day be put back in the Rotunda of the U.S. Capitol Building in Washington, D.C. This statue was carved out of an eight-ton block of marble. It is of Susan B. Anthony, Lucretia Mott, and Elizabeth Cady Stanton. Once known as the Portrait Monument, the statue was originally dedicated in the Capitol Rotunda in 1921, but days later it was put into a storage room in the basement of the building. Over the years different groups tried to get the statue raised up to be among the statues of George Washington, Abraham Lincoln, Martin Luther King, Jr., and other great American men who also built this nation. Thanks to the work of the National Museum of Women's History and thousands of women and men, this finally happened in spring 1997. This statue is the first one of American women to be honored with a place in the Rotunda. I hope that whenever girls visit the nation's capital they will stop by the Rotunda to say "hello and thank you" to Susan B. Anthony, Lucretia Mott, and my great-great-great-grandmother.

A copy of the family photo that appears on page 102 has been placed beneath the statue, along with a Susan B. Anthony dollar, in keeping with a tradition of placing artifacts under statues for future generations to find. The sculptress, Adelaide Johnson, designed the statue with uncarved marble in the background to represent generations of women to come.

ride the
wave

by Isabel Carter Stewart

When I was growing up, I had two maxims from my mother drummed into my head. If I could still talk to Momma I would tell her that she was absolutely right about one of them and that the other one, in my view, needs work.

Keep your wits about you!

This one works. I heard it countless times as I went off to school, to a party, or on a trip. By wits, she meant intellect, street smarts, and something we all come to treasure in time, humor. I know now, too, that she meant things gathered up from the ancestors: the just plain mother wit and common sense that can keep you centered and focused on your capabilities, your possibilities, your healthy self, your sanity, and ultimately the celebration of your life.

Don't go out above your knees!

This is the one that needs work. It was my mother's caution to me on those rare and special occasions when, as a very excited little girl, I got to go to the beach in the summer. I was a fledgling swimmer, and my mother did not swim at all. The ocean held an additional terror for her, I now realize, driven by her awareness that she could not save me if I got into difficulty in deep water. She was fearful for me and could not conceive of my taking on something that she herself could not. She could not imagine me learning what she didn't know, going to places she never would set foot in, or questioning traditions that, to her, were tried and true.

And so I had drummed into me, "Don't go out above your knees," which I heard as Don't be a risktaker (even an informed one)! Don't be adventuresome! Don't be so audacious as to learn to swim very well so that the water will hold no fear whatsoever for you.

Even as I maintain that Momma's second admonition does indeed need work, I understand where she was coming from. Simple survival as a woman of color was *the* issue when she was growing up in the 1920s. As a divorced mother raising her only daughter on a modest teacher's salary, she was in her own way strong, smart, and bold. I honor my mother and women like her.

I come from a tradition of resilient women, reaching back to my great-great-grandmother, whose roots I have traced to a plantation in North Carolina. I have pursued education, finding challenge and support in female-focused environments from high school through college to ten years on the campus of Spelman College as an "adult learner." (I am the spouse of Spelman's last male president.) In 1991, I joined a youth-development organization called Girls Incorporated as a staff member. Our mottos are that growing up is serious business and that girls everywhere, even beyond our one thousand program sites across the country, need to become strong, smart, and bold young women.

Girls Incorporated Girls' Bill of Rights

• Girls have a right to be themselves—people first and females second—and to resist pressure to behave in sex-stereotyped ways.
• Girls have a right to express themselves with originality and enthusiasm.
• Girls have a right to take risks, to strive freely, and to take pride in success.
• Girls have a right to accept and enjoy the bodies they were born with and not to feel pressured to compromise their health in order to satisfy the dictates of an "ideal" physical image.
• Girls have a right to be free of vulnerability and self-doubt and to develop as mentally and emotionally sound individuals.
• Girls have a right to prepare for interesting work and economic independence.

© 1992 by Girls Incorporated. All rights reserved. Reprinted with permission of Girls Incorporated.

Two generations later, I know that I must translate my mother's urgent admonition from the context of her generation and her times to mine and to yours. I know now, as we approach the next century, that if girls and young women are not challenged to go out above their knees—to be informed risktakers, to develop skills toward confidence, strength, audacity—we will not be able to act on the declaration that women's rights (and girls' rights) are human rights. We will not provide leadership or choose values that will endure. We will not effectively change the world for the benefit of all humankind.

Finally, if I were able to talk to my mother now . . .

Momma, if she had not, in the end, dared to go into the water above her knees, your daughter would not have had the courage to put these words on paper—to congratulate you on the admonition you got right and challenge the one that needed work.

I would tell her, too, that the best news is this: There are many more girls and young women today who are ready and eager to ride the waves, to do the work needed to invent themselves and create their own futures, ready and eager to make a difference and work for positive change, all the while keeping their wits about them.

25

GET TOGETHER TO GET POWER

by Faith Ringgold

O nce upon a time our planet was ruled by five great queens. During their long reign there had never been a war or a famine. Everyone was healthy, happy, and literate. All had satisfying work, a good home, and a loving family. Even the Supreme Powers of Nature who control the earth, wind, fire, rain, sun, and sea paid tribute to the Five Queens by forgoing all earthquakes, storms, forest fires, heat waves, floods, and droughts. Everything everywhere was calm and pleasant. For the first time in known history Planet Earth was at peace.

Until one day the earth erupted into chaos when the Five Daughter Queens, feeling in a competitive, playful mood, asked the question, "Which one of the Five Queens is the most powerful advocate for peace and therefore the ultimate role model for future queens?"

The Five Queens attempted to avoid answering the question. But their silence only served to kindle public interest, sparking numerous heated debates—all of which revealed that, according to the people, the Five Queens were equally powerful.

To put the issue to rest they decided to let a jury determine once and for all which one of them had made the supreme contribution toward lasting peace and therefore had the greatest power. One by one each queen came before the jury.

he first to speak was Queen Sister Soul, the awesome queen of the South. "I am a master of all the arts as well as a record-breaking athlete," she began. "Since the beginning of time, human beings have had a natural urge to celebrate their existence through creativity and to exercise their minds and bodies through sports and games. Being an artist is both a search for truth and an expression of life and beauty. My festivals of sports and games bring people from all over the planet together for peaceful competition. With all due respect to my four queen sisters, I am indisputably the most powerful."

"I am far more powerful," proclaimed Queen Sister Scholar, the brilliant queen of the West. "I am a scientist, philosopher, historian, and critic. My innovative ideas and great intellect have created this peaceful society. There is no body of knowledge or thought that is unknown to me. I have studied all scientific and technological experimentation and researched its data. I have analyzed the rise and fall of the world's great empires and through this information I have structured a workable process for world peace. Knowledge is the prime power for peace and tranquillity."

"Without justice, peace and tranquillity cannot exist," announced Queen Sister Justice, the eloquent queen of the North. "My justice system focuses on true equality of opportunity—in education, in the workplace, and in all other areas of life. I have created year-round schools and camps where our ancestors had prisons and detention centers. There are no more terrorists, drug rings, thieves, or murderers to plague our peaceful planet."

"You are all important, but I am totally essential," asserted the assiduous queen of the East, Queen Sister Work. "I produce, distribute, and service everything you need to live. I am the source of all commerce, trade, and employment. Without me, what would you eat? What would you wear?

And how would you pay for it? Work is at the center of life as we know it. If we didn't have work, how long would we have peace?"

The last to speak was Queen Sister Family, the imperious queen of the vast central region. "Listen to me, my dear sisters," she commanded, "I am the one who binds you together. I specialize in love, faith, patience, and understanding. I speak for the children, the old, the indigent, and the sick. I give you security, love, and support. I am the guardian of the culture—your personal history and identity. No matter who you are or what you have, you need me. I truly love you, my dear sister queens, but my superior position of power is undeniable."

The jury, made up of men and women from all five regions, listened to the debate but was deadlocked.

In desperation, the Five Daughter Queens turned to their fathers, the Five Husbands.

"We know a powerful woman when we see one," boasted the Five Husbands in unison. "You have come to the right place."

"Well, tell us," pleaded the Five Daughter Queens, "which of our mothers is the most powerful and the ultimate role model?"

The Five Husbands began arguing the merits of their wives' personal power.

"My wife, the awesome Queen Sister Soul, is not only a master artist and athlete but also a veritable fashion plate!" thundered Husband One.

"It is my wife, the elegant and charming Queen Sister Scholar, who is the most powerful," bellowed Husband Two.

"There is no truth among you," screamed Husband Three. "Queen Sister Justice is so sexy that grown men become speechless in her presence."

"Stop pretending," pleaded Husband Four. "The obvious choice is my wife, Queen Sister Work, who is much prettier and more youthful than any of your wives. The power of womanhood at its finest is manifest in her flawless complexion and her big brown eyes."

"It is a disgrace to distort the truth," growled Husband Five. "It is my wife, Queen Sister Family, who is the most beautiful and loving, and . . . "

Soon their fiery debate turned violent when each husband fabricated stories about the others' wives' questionable character, false charm, and artificial good looks. At that point the Five Husbands drew their weapons—secretly loaded after all these years—and opened fire.

Fortunately no one was killed, but some innocent bystanders were wounded. And the planet had heard its first gunshots since the Five Queens began their reign. Everyone everywhere took sides, and battles broke out all around.

he Supreme Powers of Nature, so long blissful, released an urgent message to all concerned, demanding an immediate peaceful resolution. But the Five Queens and their husbands ignored the message and continued to fight. And so did everybody else. Without further warning, the Supreme Powers of Nature sent a torrent of freezing rain and hurricane winds cascading across the earth, covering it with frost and sheets of ice. When they saw that people kept fighting anyway, the Supreme Powers of Nature produced a heat wave, which melted the ice and frost and flooded the planet. But still the fighting continued. So next the Supreme Powers of Nature stopped all precipitation and dried up all the oceans, rivers, and streams, creating a drought that parched the earth and destroyed its crops, thereby producing a dreaded famine. The entire planet was nearly a wasteland.

Finally the Five Queens, their husbands, and all the people on the planet stood still and heard the message of the Supreme Powers of Nature:

> **The Five Queens' personal beauty, elegance, and charm have nothing to do with peace or power. And further, *individual power* is no power at all. The Five Queens created a world at peace through collaboration. *Each* has made an invaluable contribution to life and peace on earth. However, their foolish quest for power has reduced this once-peaceful planet to hell on earth. The Five Queens must step down and concede to the Five Daughter Queens before any more harm is done.**

Thus each Daughter Queen became ruler of her mother's region, and all was peaceful for many years until, alas, the day came when the Five Daughter Queens had daughters of their own. Those Five Granddaughter Queens grew up and asked that haunting question: "Which one of the Five Daughter Queens is the most powerful advocate for peace and therefore the ultimate role model for future queens?" As soon as the question hit the air, a wind of hurricane force blew across the earth with a vengeance.

In the distance the sun was grinning as the Five Daughter Queens promptly spoke these words:

> **"Darling daughters, we have only this to say about power:
> None of us is more powerful than the unity of our combined
> resources. If we use our power to compete with one another,
> we will lose everything. All of us working together, in harmony
> with the Supreme Powers of Nature, is the essence of world
> power, peace, and tranquillity."**

"Aaaamen! Aaaamen! Aaaamen! Dear daughters!" the Five Queens cried out. "Beloved granddaughters, listen and be informed!"

And that, my dear sisters and brothers of Planet Earth, was and still is the last word.

26

DANCE TO YOUR COLORS

by Wendy Wasserstein

A friend of mine was considering sending his four-year-old daughter to a cram course for the nursery school equivalent of the Scholastic Aptitude Test. He said he couldn't imagine what his daughter's future would be if she wasn't accepted into the school of his choice. When my friend asked my advice, I found myself admitting a truth I had never before come out with publicly. I was a Dalton School reject.

I remember the humiliation as if it were yesterday and, of course, I also remember that it wasn't entirely the school's fault. If I had to take an entrance exam for the Dalton School today, there's still a good chance I would be doomed.

It happened in the spring of 1963. My family was planning to move from Brooklyn to Manhattan, and so we entered, unassuming, into the fast and fabulous world of the New York City private school system. Before the move, I was a student at the Brooklyn Ethical Culture School. There I played Portia in the eighth-grade production of *Julius Caesar* and was particularly advanced at dancing to the colors in Prospect Park. Our dance instructor, Mrs. Janovsky, would beat a tambourine as she rhythmically called out, "Red," "Yellow," "Purple," and we students would in turn express our most visceral connection to each color. It wasn't Summerhill, but it wasn't Bronx Science either.

The world of New York City private schools—Brearley, Spence, Dalton, et al.—was completely foreign to me. In fact, I thought that to have a school named after you, you had to be a president, an inventor, or have the initials P.S. Of course I also didn't know that Manhattan went so far north of Fifty-seventh Street. And I didn't realize that beyond the theater district and Macy's there was a whole residential life going on. To a born-and-bred Brooklynite, "the city" was a place where you went to shop or to take in a show, and then you went home. You certainly didn't spend the night or take a test there in the morning.

I basically believe that most of my family's impressions about schools came from my brother's opinions of the girls he met at high school dances. There was someone from Dalton who had blond, straight hair parted on the side, a mid-sixties Dorothy Lamour. And there was a young lady from Brearley who was obsessed with *The Great Gatsby*. Both of these recommendations led my mother to make inquiries.

Brearley, at the time, seemed more concerned that I hadn't studied French in elementary school than impressed with my Portia or my yellow interpretations. As I recall, my mother and I were both intimidated. We never arranged to take a tour of the school or scheduled an interview. And, in fact, my brother never actually dated the girl who was obsessed with *Gatsby*.

We did, however, pay a visit to Dalton, which in 1963 was still an all-women's school. I remember peeking into the assembly hall and counting row after row of heads with meticulously parted hair and row after row of feet with Pappagallo shoes. Surely if I went to school there I would also be able to wear those pink, paper-thin slippers in the snow.

I've never been a big fan of standardized testing. I've always felt encouraged by the story of the boy who filled out his S.A.T. answer sheet in the shape of a Christmas tree and scored a 763. Mostly what I remember of my Dalton entrance test is the blank piece of paper on which we were supposed to "be creative." Since my drawing skills were (and still are) easily outstripped by the average four-year-old, I decided to combine my literary and artistic abilities. I drew a tree and quoted Joyce Kilmer's immortal "I think that I shall never see / A poem lovely as . . . " a you know what.

As I was drawing, I looked around the room at the girls with discreet bands of silver on their fingers and decided that they all belonged to a world I wasn't part of. Though their feet were pink and preppy, they were unmistakably worldly and "artistic." Their days were no doubt filled with high-minded pastimes. They would never dance to the colors.

My family, however, became determined that I should go to Dalton. After all, I'd receive a proper education, I'd move beyond Joyce Kilmer, my brother would get invited to more high school dances and meet more girls with straight hair parted on the side, and we would quickly assimilate into Upper East Side Manhattan.

On the day of my interview at Dalton, my mother turned out in an uncharacteristically conservative suit, urgently tasteful, and I wore a turquoise mohair coat that today someone in some thrift shop on Avenue A would find divinely retro.

"So, what are your interests, dear?" An older woman in a Marimekko dress was trying to get to know me as a person.

"Well, history, theater," I answered.

"Our girls pursue many of their own interests." She went on to tell me about a girl who traveled to Egypt and was so excited by her trip that she wrote a book about it her sophomore year.

This is where the turning point came. I was twelve at the time, and I knew I could say that I wanted to choreograph my own play, write a book, pursue my own interests, but I didn't feel like it. I didn't want to be one of this woman's girls. It was that simple.

"Why do you want to come to Dalton, dear?" She was working the room. Trying to get a conversation going.

I surreptitiously put a piece of gum in my mouth and began chewing.

My mother turned to me. "Honey, tell her why you want to go to Dalton."

"I don't," I blurted out with the thickest Brooklyn accent imaginable. The Lords of Flatbush had nothing on me. I continued chewing and even burst a tiny bubble. "Look, lady, I want to go to public school with my friends."

Now I might have been a Dalton reject even if I hadn't delivered that statement. The Joyce Kilmer sketch alone probably would have been sufficient cause for exclusion. But my mother will never forget that moment. Her hope for me, her great expectations, went soaring out the window.

Shortly afterward I began behaving myself at school interviews. And I was accepted at the Calhoun School, which was also an all-women's school at the time. The girls there wore Pappagallos, too. But Calhoun did not have the cachet of Dalton. I remember how the mother of my high school boyfriend (he was very smart and went to Horace Mann) was always slightly miffed at his choice of lady friend. After all, both of his sisters attended Dalton.

It's twenty-five years now since my high school interviews. And the world and I have both completely evolved. I know this because I recently had an opportunity to spend an evening with the headmistress of Brearley.

When, at dinner, the headmistress of Brearley asked me where I went to high school, I immediately responded that I had graduated from Mount Holyoke. When she asked again, I covered my mouth and whispered, "Calhoun."

The truth is, I really wanted to put a stick of gum in my mouth and belt, "Look, lady, for your information, I was a Dalton reject." But instead I was well behaved. In part, I suppose, because there might come a day when I'll be dragging my own daughter to an interview at Brearley. Here's hoping she won't take after her mother.

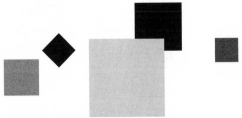

27

remem
BELIEVE.
a

by Bernice Johnson Reagon (Mother)
& Toshi Reagon (Daughter)

BERNICE: It was spring 1953 and I was ten years old. I had just graduated from the seventh grade at Blue Spring Elementary School, a red one-room schoolhouse in Dougherty County, Georgia. What was exciting about passing to the eighth grade was that I would be going to Carver Junior High School in "town." I was excited and I was scared. I lived in the country, and "town"—Albany, Georgia, the county seat of Dougherty—was big. Blue Spring Elementary had between thirty and forty students, first through seventh grade. Carver Junior High, which was the junior high school for all African Americans in Dougherty County, was really big. I did not know anything about the city except that I had heard that city kids were big and rough.

The only way to get to Carver Junior High was on a bus. It was a very big deal for Black people in Dougherty County, Georgia. White children had been bused to schools in town for a long time, but it was very difficult for Black people to get buses. My father, Reverend Jessie Johnson, and my uncle, Elijah Williams, went to the school superintendent and asked for a bus so that those of us who lived in the country could have transportation to continue school after seventh grade. Until that happened,

118

after elementary school, if you were Black, you had several choices. If your family had a car and you had a driver's license, you could drive to school every day. If your parents could afford it, or if you had relatives in town, you could stay in town and go on to school that way. Or you could go to work in the fields farming, or do domestic work, or yard work—for the rest of your life.

By the time I finished seventh grade, because of my father and my uncle, I was riding on a bus to go to school. It was great! Because of this experience I have always known all the stuff against busing was a cover for racism because everybody in our community—Black and White—wanted to be bused to go to the city schools so that you could continue your education.

At Carver everybody kept asking me how old I was. I was ten and small. They would look down at me and say, "You must be smart, hunh?" I had two girlfriends who were the right age to be in the eighth grade. They were short and closer to my size. But when they got their period, they changed. They were quieter, sometimes they wouldn't feel good, they walked differently—slower. They did not giggle and run down the hall as much. It felt like everybody had their period but me, or at least they had it before the end of that year. And they all wore stockings and lipstick. Every last one of them! But not me. My mother wouldn't hear of it. No stockings, no lipstick, no earrings, and of course, absolutely no heels! It didn't matter that I was in junior high school.

There was one other student as small as me at Carver. His name was Charles Barber—my first boyfriend.

This situation—being too young, smart, and physically small—stayed with me as I moved on to senior high in 1954. Near the end of my year at Carver, my cousin Johnny drove me over to Monroe Senior High. He introduced me to one of his friends as an honor student who would be going to Monroe in the fall. His friend asked me how old I was. "Twelve," I replied. (Well, I was almost twelve. At least by that October, I would be twelve.)

He said, "Man, am I glad I am graduating from this place." It seemed to me that he thought the worst thing in the world that could happen to him was if he had to still be in high school with people like me coming in—out of time, out of place.

This was the fifties in Southwest Georgia and the beginning of my coming to myself as a fighter in the Freedom Movement. The absolutely most important thing that happened to me during the 1950s was Autherine Lucy. Autherine Lucy was the first Black person to attend the University of Alabama. She applied during the fall of 1952, when I was in the seventh grade, and was admitted by court order through the work of the NAACP, on January 30, 1956, when I was in the tenth grade. When Autherine Lucy entered the University of Alabama, I went with her. In my mind, in my spirit, I went with her.

Autherine Lucy was my model. Everyone needs one. I was going to my classes every day, but in my spirit, I went to the University of Alabama with Autherine Lucy—following her story in the newspapers, on the radio, and on television. When the Board of Trustees put her out, they put me out. When her attorney, Thurgood Marshall of the NAACP Legal Defense and Educational Fund, got her back in—I went in with her. When she was suspended again, I was just waiting for Attorney Marshall to get us back in, and before I knew it, Autherine Lucy had gone and married a preacher! I was stunned! I was just getting started!

Learning that human models can't keep up with the fantasy you create in your head is hard. It broke my heart. I was left with going to school, going to church, singing in the gospel choir, being with my sisters and brothers, being short, small, and smart—and waiting for the next fight. Next time it would not be just in my mind. The next time it would be all of me. Autherine Lucy had shown me the way. Somehow I was going to be in the number, fighting for myself and my people. I couldn't wait. But I had to—I was still trying to be thirteen years old.

I still long to see my early idol face to face and tell her what she did for me—a small, short, smart Black girl looking for who she could be in this world. She helped me to locate myself. I thank you for the journey, Ms. Autherine Lucy Foster, and I forgive you for getting married on me.

TOSHI: When I was four I said my first curse word. A real one, not like "stupid." My brother and I were not allowed to say stupid. The word I said was "damn."

I was coming home from preschool or something on this April day in 1968, walking up toward my home, which stood at the top of a hill. There were thousands of people and police everywhere. I asked, "What's going on?" They told me Martin Luther King was dead. Someone had killed him. And I said "Damn!"

The funeral procession went right down our street. It looked like every kind of police or army man ever known was there. It felt like the whole thing was centered at my house. I was scared, but the tone in the air was not of fear—at least not to my four-year-old senses. I remember being fired up and wanting to change the world.

Mom was, and is, a great example to me. She is a great singer, and when my brother, Kwan, and I were little, she took us everywhere—to festivals and concert halls, churches, and protest rallies. It was great! I knew at an early age that my mother was special, and worked very hard. I can see now how she was able to accomplish so much. She had a way of breaking down any task into steps and then dealing with each one without focusing on the end result—just concentrating on the first step, the second step, the next . . . until she reached the end.

In 1971, when I was seven, Mom moved us to Washington, D.C., where she worked at the D.C. Repertory Theatre Company and attended Howard University to get her Ph.D. That was a cool year because I saw the Jackson Five in Atlanta before we moved. Michael Jackson, ten years old, singing and dancing with his brothers—I remember every move of that concert! They were hotter than the group Immature is now.

Three days after arriving in D.C., I got into a running competition with another kid. I was speeding down the hill toward my apartment building. There was an iron fence at the bottom of the hill. I was running so fast, I was scared I wouldn't be able to stop. I saw the fence. It was about three and a half feet high. "I can jump that," I thought. I ran faster, and . . . my right foot got caught, and *smack,* I went face first onto the cement. I broke my front tooth. Over the next three years, I broke that tooth six times.

We went to school in Northwest Washington, close to Howard, but we lived in Anacostia, in Southeast D.C. My mom picked a school near hers that had no broken windows in it during the summer (Anacostia was a bit on the rough side), and so I had to take two buses to get home. I did not like it then, and now I hate looking back on those memories. Even today it is really hard for me to get on a bus.

But I did like school, not so much the work but rather the community of school. I was good at sports and was what they called in less liberated times a tomboy. I was always different from my classmates. I got along better with boys than with girls. I got picked on a lot for my differences—everything from developing breasts before everyone else to leaving my hair natural. Well, I started to fight back, and before I knew it I had a reputation for kicking butt. No, violence was not the answer, but because I was afraid of getting beat up, I let my reputation live. I didn't have to fight much after a while.

When I was twelve, I hurt my right hip playing football. My sports injury led me to have four operations between the ages of twelve and twenty on that same hip. Yet when I look back on it all, it amazes me how fast I adjusted to the changes the injury and the operations would cause in my life. For one, no longer able to run, I had to give up my dream of becoming the first female quarterback in the National Football League. I turned to music. Boom! Just like that. I am writing this while recuperating from my sixth surgery—same hip, and it was so hard for me to deal with. I had to go into training to survive the ordeal, and every possible fear that could come up, did.

When I was fifteen, a lot of great things happened to me. I got truly serious about my music and pretty much decided that songwriting, singing, and playing instruments would be what I would do for the rest of my life. Also, I came out. Yeah, I had my first girlfriend. It was cool. Lucky for me, I went to a school where it wasn't a big deal. Most people my age were straight, but I knew some students were experimenting with their sexuality. It was a real gift to be able to feel comfortable about myself.

I was doing something that society as a whole did not approve of. Although I had great friends at school, I went looking for other gay people to be with. Community is so important, and sometimes you have to be creative in building one. Now I feel I have the best friends in the world. We all come from different places and differ in age, race, religion, class, and sexuality. I love getting a discussion going and hearing many points of view. When one of us has a problem, I love the creative responses we bring to addressing the issue.

I don't feel that people should be the same. I believe that we should find a way to live with and even embrace what we find different in each other. It's good. Sometimes I look at the differences between people and how they are sometimes used to create hostilities, and it scares me. I wonder if conditions, as we near the end of the twentieth century, could separate our diverse community or push us down. When faced with fear, I try to remember my mother's steps, and I try to find that four-year-old-girl energy that got me to say "Damn!" and then I continue to change the world. Thanks, Mom.

BERNICE: The first time I cursed, I was eight years old. I had washed a pair of white socks. I had used bleach, so the socks were whiter than white. I decided to carry them out to the clothesline in the last rinse water. So I got a pail of water, put the white socks in, and went to the line. I sat the pail on the ground and tiptoed up to get the clothespins off the line. Just then one of our pigs came by, rooting its nose to the ground, and knocked over the pail. My white socks spilled into the now-muddy earth. I said "Shit!" Out loud.

I looked around to see if anybody heard me. My heart was beating so fast. I had never said a curse word before. I never knew they could fly out of your mouth at intense times and cut the air like that. It was then that I began to understand that there were a lot of things I knew: words, things I had overheard, things that never—or almost never—left my mouth. By the way, nobody heard me—so I lived to tell this story.

Sometimes when you do something that is out of the ordinary for you—it is, but it does not have to become your name: You can rinse the mud out of your socks, remember not to take them to the line in a pail of water, watch out for the pig, and go on with your life.

28

ELE

by Sandra Cisneros

What they don't understand about birthdays and what they never tell you is that when you're eleven, you're also ten, and nine, and eight, and seven, and six, and five, and four, and three, and two, and one. And when you wake up on your eleventh birthday you expect to feel eleven, but you don't. You open your eyes and everything's just like yesterday, only it's today. And you don't feel eleven at all. You feel like you're still ten. And you are—underneath the year that makes you eleven.

Like some days when you might say something stupid, and that's the part of you that's still ten. Or maybe some days you might need to sit on your mama's lap because you're scared, and that's the part of you that's five. And maybe one day when you're all grown up maybe you will need to cry like if you're three, and that's okay. That's what I tell Mama when she's sad and needs to cry. Maybe she's feeling three.

Because the way you grow old is kind of like an onion or like the rings inside a tree trunk or like my little wooden dolls that fit one inside the other, each year inside the next one. That's how being eleven years old is.

You don't feel eleven. Not right away. It takes a few days, weeks even, sometimes even months before you say Eleven when they ask you. And you

VEN

(is more than ten plus one)

don't feel smart eleven, not until you're almost twelve. That's the way it is.

Only today I wish I didn't have only eleven years rattling inside me like pennies in a tin Band-Aid box. Today I wish I was one hundred and two instead of eleven because if I was one hundred and two I'd have known what to say when Mrs. Price put the red sweater on my desk. I would've known how to tell her it wasn't mine instead of just sitting there with that look on my face and nothing coming out of my mouth.

"Whose is this?" Mrs. Price says, and she holds the red sweater up in the air for all the class to see. "Whose? It's been sitting in the coatroom for a month."

"Not mine," says everybody. "Not me."

"It has to belong to somebody," Mrs. Price keeps saying, but nobody can remember. It's an ugly sweater with red plastic buttons and a collar and sleeves all stretched out like you could use it for a jump rope. It's maybe a thousand years old and even if it belonged to me I wouldn't say so.

Maybe because I'm skinny, maybe because she doesn't like me, that stupid Sylvia Saldívar says, "I think it belongs to Rachel." An ugly sweater like that, all raggedy and old, but Mrs. Price believes her. Mrs. Price takes the sweater and puts it right on my desk, but when I open my mouth nothing comes out.

"That's not, I don't, you're not . . . Not mine," I finally say in a little voice that was maybe me when I was four.

"Of course it's yours," Mrs. Price says. "I remember you wearing it once." Because she's older and the teacher, she's right and I'm not.

Not mine, not mine, not mine, but Mrs. Price is already turning to page thirty-two, and math problem number four. I don't know why but all of a sudden I'm feeling sick inside, like the part of me that's three wants to come out of my eyes, only I squeeze them shut tight and bite down on my teeth real hard and try to remember today I am eleven, eleven. Mama is making a cake for me for tonight, and when Papa comes home everybody will sing Happy birthday, happy birthday to you.

But when the sick feeling goes away and I open my eyes, the red sweater's still sitting there like a big red mountain. I move the red sweater to the corner of my desk with my ruler. I move my pencil and books and eraser as far from it as possible. I even move my chair a little to the right. Not mine, not mine, not mine.

In my head I'm thinking how long till lunchtime, how long till I can take the red sweater and throw it over the schoolyard fence, or leave it hanging on a parking meter, or bunch it up into a little ball and toss it in the alley. Except when math period ends Mrs. Price says loud and in front of everybody, "Now, Rachel, that's enough," because she sees I've shoved the red sweater to the tippy-tip corner of my desk and it's hanging all over the edge like a waterfall, but I don't care.

"Rachel," Mrs. Price says. She says it like she's getting mad. "You put that sweater on right now and no more nonsense."

"But it's not—"

"Now!" Mrs. Price says.

This is when I wish I wasn't eleven, because all the years inside of me—ten, nine, eight, seven, six, five, four, three, two, and one—are pushing at the back of my eyes when I put one arm through one sleeve of the sweater that smells like cottage cheese, and then the other arm through the other and stand there with my arms apart like if the sweater hurts me and it does, all itchy and full of germs that aren't even mine.

That's when everything I've been holding in since this morning, since when Mrs. Price put the sweater on my desk, finally lets go, and all of a sudden I'm crying in front of everybody. I wish I was invisible but I'm not. I'm eleven and it's my birthday today and I'm crying like I'm three in front of everybody. I put my head down on the desk and bury my face in my stupid clown-sweater arms. My face all hot and spit coming out of my mouth because I can't stop the little animal noises from coming out of me, until there aren't any more tears left in my eyes, and it's just my body shaking like when you have the hiccups, and my whole head hurts like when you drink milk too fast.

But the worst part is right before the bell rings for lunch. That stupid Phyllis Lopez, who is even dumber than Sylvia Saldívar, says she remembers the red sweater is hers! I take it off right away and give it to her, only Mrs. Price pretends like everything's okay.

Today I'm eleven. There's a cake Mama's making for tonight, and when Papa comes home from work we'll eat it. There'll be candles and presents and everybody will sing Happy birthday, happy birthday to you, Rachel, only it's too late.

I'm eleven today. I'm eleven, ten, nine, eight, seven, six, five, four, three, two, and one, but I wish I was one hundred and two. I wish I was anything but eleven, because I want today to be far away already, far away like a runaway balloon, like a tiny *o* in the sky, so tiny-tiny you have to close your eyes to see it.

by Lynda Barry

nothing is as healing as a book

by Alice Hoffman

When I was a child, I was convinced that something miraculous was about to happen. I lived a very ordinary and very unhappy life, yet I was certain that at any moment all that would change. It was an everyday possibility, this miracle of mine. It could happen any time, while I buttered toast in the kitchen or played kickball out on the street. Birthdays came and went, but I wasn't worried. I never wavered in my belief. Sooner or later I'd meet up with my destiny, and time didn't matter, at least not back then. If I could wait the eight or nine years until I was old enough for a driver's license, well, then I could most assuredly wait for a miracle as well.

My fortune seemed most likely to improve on those afternoons when I walked to the library in the next town. The route I took was a green, leafy path, so removed from the asphalt of our neighborhood, so overgrown with weeds it was almost possible to forget the leaves hid a chain-link fence and that it wasn't a river flowing on the other side of the fence but rather the start of rush-hour traffic on the Southern State Parkway. Each day as I set out from home I was confident this was to be the hour of my miracle, and when it did not happen, I refused to be disappointed. Frankly, I'd been disappointed enough.

By the age of seven I'd discovered that families don't necessarily stay together. By eight I'd found out that those who vow they will love you forever can easily disappear. By nine I knew that even when your mother kissed you good night and promised you'd sleep tight, she herself might be up till all hours worrying about those problems that so plague grownups—food and laundry, dollars and cents, love and agony.

No matter what grownups may say, children know there are monsters in the world. They may not be in the closet or under the bed, but they're there all the same. They're on the street corner, robbing you on your way home from school. They're walking the avenues with matches, guns, and knives. They're in the boys' room and the girls' room at school, on the other side of the window or below the sink. They're in a teacher's heart, an uncle's hands. They're your meanest brother, the one who won't leave you alone. They're you sometimes, the way you feel inside.

Facts are facts: the monsters are, were, and always will be there. But to me it seemed only fair that there be miracles as well. As it turned out, there were, although it was years before I realized that my miracle had been happening all along. It wasn't an amulet, which would grant three wishes, or a beast who could speak, or a rose that would never die. It was the best sort of miracle, the kind that happens when the heat outside is blistering or when a storm is brewing: when everything in your life is out of your control. It happens when you are eight, or ten, or twelve, at the moment when you discover that when you walk into a library, you have complete freedom. You can leave your world behind and enter into any book you select. Here, where there is quiet, there are, at last, choices to be made. No one will tell you what to believe or how to feel. Best of all: no one will tell you what you can and cannot imagine.

I think now that I would not have survived my childhood if not for those walks to the library. Books were the true miracle in my life, my salvation and my ticket out—a blessing I'm grateful for every single day. Nothing is as intimate, as healing, as private as a book.

Often the people who succeed, in spite of the difficulties they may face, have one thing in common. They read. They are the people who can escape into a book, who know there are other worlds to be found. They are the ones who carry books with them to movie theaters and street corners, who lock themselves in the bathroom to read when everyone in the house is too noisy, who open a new chapter when the world outside their windows is too horrible or disappointing or simply too fast. They have hope because they know that once upon a time there was a boy or a girl, a woman or a man, who managed to survive. Somewhere, among the pages and the print, there was someone who found solace or justice or truth, or maybe just a chance to tell her own story.

HELP IS OUT THERE

by Mavis Jukes

Our number one "hope and help" line is the communication we have with caring family members. Talking to parents, guardians, and other responsible adults helps keep kids safe and strong.

But sometimes preteens and teens encounter situations in which they need help, information, or advice beyond or in addition to what is available from the people around them. **No one should feel lost or alone with a problem—especially not a kid.** That's one reason why youth hotlines have been established.

> Before you read about the **Hotlines** below, take a minute to remind yourself that if you or anyone else is in immediate danger, the number to call is: **the police emergency number.** Dial **911** or **0** for the operator—and tell the person who answers what kind of help you need.

WHAT EXACTLY IS A HOTLINE?

A hotline is a telephone number that people call for help, information, or advice. Hotlines are set up so that:

1. A kid can talk to a helpful and understanding adult volunteer—or professional counselor—about problems, *big* or small.

2. A kid can get questions answered *privately* about a variety of topics related to health—like information about sexually transmitted diseases.

3. A kid in need can get hooked up with services in his or her own community, such as family counselors or youth support groups, drug and alcohol rehab programs, other health care providers, and government agencies that protect kids from abuse or neglect.

Anyone can call a youth hotline; sometimes adults call, to find out ways to help their kids, their kids' friends, their families, or themselves.

BUT HOW DO YOU FIND OUT THE HOTLINE NUMBERS?

Hotline numbers are usually listed in the first few pages at the front of the phone book. They may also be listed in the white pages. The information operator **(411)** can also provide hotline numbers. Some hotline numbers can be found by calling **1-800-555-1212,** which is the information number for free calls even if they are long distance.

But it's a really good idea to memorize at least one 24-hour, seven-day-a-week national youth hotline number, and this one is surely the easiest to remember: **THE COVENANT HOUSE NINE LINE: 1-800-999-9999.**

Dialing **1-800, 1-888,** or **1-877** before a seven-digit telephone number means the call doesn't cost anything, no matter how long you talk. It doesn't appear on the phone bill.

These numbers can be dialed from any phone, including a pay phone— without charge. If you have trouble getting through, dial 0 and the operator can help you make the connection.

YOUTH CRISIS HOTLINES

The following national youth crisis hotlines are available 24 hours a day, seven days a week. Remember: Parents and other family members—and anyone else—can call, too.

1. THE COVENANT HOUSE 9 LINE (U.S. ONLY): **1-800-999-9999.** Remember? Just think 9!

2. THE BOYS TOWN NATIONAL HOTLINE isn't just for boys—it's for girls, too. It's a youth crisis hotline, so anyone can call about any problem. But it's also important to know that the adults who answer the phone calls have some *extra-special* training in suicide prevention. **BOYS TOWN NATIONAL HOTLINE** (ENGLISH AND SPANISH): **1-800-448-3000** (U.S. AND CANADA); FOR THE HEARING IMPAIRED: **1-800-448-1833 (TDD)**

> ➤ A person who is thinking about ending his or her own life needs help right away. The way to help someone who is feeling suicidal is to tell a responsible adult about the situation. Don't keep the secret.
> **Remember: In an emergency, call 911 or 0 and tell the person who answers what kind of help you need.**

3. THE RUNAWAY HOTLINES

Yes, some kids experience situations such as abuse, a serious breakdown of communication with parents, conflicts within the family, or other stressful situations that make them feel as if they can't cope if they remain at home.

But running away to the streets *isn't a solution.* It exposes kids to crime and violence, hunger, disease, and people who prey on kids.

There are agencies and support groups set up to help kids and their families find safe solutions to problems at home within their own communities. Sometimes it's in the kid's best interest for alternate living arrangements to be made, either on a temporary or a permanent basis.

These arrangements need to be made by responsible adults who are in a position to safeguard a child's health and well-being.

THE NATIONAL RUNAWAY SWITCHBOARD is a youth crisis hotline for kids who are thinking about running away, for kids who have already run away, or for kids who want to talk about other problems—including having a friend who has run away or who is planning to. The number is: **1-800-621-4000** (U.S. ONLY); FOR THE HEARING IMPAIRED: **1-800-621-0394 (TDD).**

Every community wants missing children returned—no matter how far they may be away from home, no matter how long they've been gone, and no matter what has happened to them while they were gone. There is a national center set up to help all runaway, missing, lost, abandoned, or abducted children. **THE NATIONAL CENTER FOR MISSING AND EXPLOITED CHILDREN HOTLINE** NUMBER IS: **1-800-843-5678** (U.S. AND CANADA); FOR THE HEARING IMPAIRED, THE NUMBER IS: **1-800-826-7653 (TDD)**. **CHILD HELP U.S.A.** *Child Help U.S.A. is never closed and the lines are answered by professional counselors. The number is easy to remember.* It's **1-800-4-A-CHILD (1-800-422-4453)**;(U.S. AND CANADA) FOR THE HEARING IMPAIRED: **1-800-2-A-CHILD (TDD) (1-800-222-4453)(TDD)**. (The numbers on a phone usually have letters on them, too. After dialing 1-800, dial 4—and then just press the numbers that have the letters that spell out "A CHILD.")

➤ Confused about what hotline number to call in a given situation?
Any youth crisis hotline will work—just call and someone will listen and direct you.

This hotline can be called anytime by anybody who has a question, concern, or problem involving *any* kind of abuse, including physical abuse, emotional abuse, neglect, or sexual abuse.

SEXUAL ABUSE—SPECIAL ALERT

Kids almost always have an instinctive feeling that something is wrong when an adult or significantly older kid tries to talk to them or touch them in a sexual way. It seems wrong—because it *is* wrong.

Even a young kid can have enormous power against a person who attempts abuse. The power lies in trusting the feeling that something is wrong, saying *no!* and reporting what happened right away. A kid should *not* be polite to an adult who tries to interest him or her in sex and should *not* keep the adult's problem a secret, even if the person with the problem happens to be in a position of trust or power, such as a family friend, camp counselor, coach, religious leader, teacher, family member, or parent.

Kids *cannot* get in trouble for reporting, although many child abusers lie to a kid and say that the kid will be blamed. Some try to pretend it's the kid's fault—but it's *never* the kid's fault, and all adults know this. Some abusers threaten kids, and try to make them afraid to tell. Anyone who is being threatened by someone is much safer when other people know about the threats.

Who should a kid tell?

Any trusted adult should be told—like a parent, another adult relative, a teacher, principal, school counselor, health care giver, police officer, or firefighter, or a counselor who answers the Child Help U.S.A. Hotline.

QUESTIONS?

Never hesitate to call the Child Help U.S.A. Hotline (numbers above) with questions or concerns about abuse. You may have to wait for a minute or two.

But don't hang up.

A counselor will come on the line.

WHAT ABOUT A HOTLINE ABOUT DRUG AND ALCOHOL PROBLEMS?

Everyone must *learn* to deal with stress, frustration, anxiety, and other uncomfortable feelings. Those who use drugs to try to make stressful feelings go away don't confront the feelings and don't develop good strategies for dealing with life's challenges. As a result, teens who routinely use alcohol, marijuana, or other drugs can impair their development into confident adults.

Illegal drug use can cause addiction and permanent physical damage, including brain damage. Through sharing equipment used to inject drugs, a person can contract diseases, including AIDS. There's also the possibility of death through overdose.

Anyone, including a teen, who has a problem with drugs or alcohol can get help without getting in trouble for admitting underage drinking or illegal substance use.

THE NATIONAL COUNCIL ON ALCOHOLISM AND DRUG DEPENDENCE HOPE LINE NUMBER IS: **1-800-622-2255** (U.S. AND CANADA). This isn't a 24-hour, seven-day-a-week hotline, but there's always a message saying when you can call back.

Too much alcohol can cause the brain to stop giving out signals telling the lungs to breathe, which leads to the heart stopping beating. Too much alcohol can cause someone to pass out or fail to wake up or be woken up. A person who is passed out may throw up while asleep and choke on the vomit. A person may be awake but still be unable to keep from choking on vomit. Someone in a condition described above needs *someone to call the police emergency number immediately!* **(911 OR 0 FOR THE OPERATOR)**

*If a drunk person's safety seems in jeopardy for **any** reason, get help from a responsible, sober adult—without hesitating. Don't worry about whether the drunk person might get into trouble for drinking. Just get help.*

➤ **News Flash:**
Alcohol use can become a medical emergency.
   Hundreds of teens die every year as a result of drinking too much alcohol at one time.

? ? ? ? ?   ? ? ? ? ?   ? ? ? ? ?   ? ? ? ? ?   ? ? ? ? ?

Teens often have questions that require more complete answers than they might get in school or at home. Have you heard people talking about HIV and other sexually transmitted diseases? Do you have questions or worries? Are you just plain curious?

Information about sexually transmitted diseases changes, but we all can stay informed and find answers to questions by calling the **CDC NATIONAL STD HOTLINE.** The number is **1-800-227-8922** (U.S. ONLY). FOR THE HEARING IMPAIRED, THE NUMBER IS: **1-800-243-7889 (TDD).**

There is also a **NATIONAL HIV/AIDS HOTLINE** (U.S. ONLY). THE NUMBER IS: **1-800-342-AIDS (2437).** FOR THE HEARING IMPAIRED, THE NUMBER IS **1-800-243-7889 (TDD).** EN ESPAÑOL: **1-800-344-7432.**

If you call when the hotline is closed, or when all the volunteers who answer the phones are talking to other people, a recording will tell you when to call back.

If a hotline number becomes unavailable, a good thing to do is dial **411** for information or **0** for the operator and ask for help finding a similar hotline listing. If you don't get a number that you need from the first operator you are connected with, hang up and try again by calling **411** or **0** for a different operator.

Don't give up.

live with a thirst

by Natalie Merchant

COUNT YOUR BREATHS

LISTEN TO THE MOTION
OF YOUR HEART

MAKE A CRADLE OF YOUR ARMS
TO HOLD YOUR BABY SISTER

FEEL YOUR MIND
LOSE ITS RESTLESSNESS

SING

SHARE LAUGHTER

CONSIDER THE DETAILS

HOW LIGHT AND SHADOW
PLAY IN THE ROOM

YOUR MOTHER'S HANDS
FOLDING LAUNDRY

THE STRENGTH
IN YOUR LIMBS

SEARCH THE NIGHT SKY
IN CLUSTERS OF WHITE LIGHT
SEE STARS
DISTANT SUNS
A VAST HEAVEN
WILL REMIND YOU
THERE IS A SCALE OF THINGS

AND DECIDE TO

STAND
FOR THE WOMAN
CARRYING HER CHILD
ON THE RUSH HOUR
CROWDED BUS

BE AWESTRUCK
BY THE STIRRING
BENEATH THE SOIL
THAT WILL PROMISE
SPRING

PREPARE AND SHARE
YOUR DAILY MEALS
WITH THE PEOPLE YOU LOVE

DESIRE PEACE
IN YOUR LIFE
AND
IN YOUR WORLD

FORGIVE WITH GRACE
LEARN WITH PATIENCE

SEEK BEAUTY

PROTECT A PLACE
IN YOURSELF
WHERE
YOUR INNOCENCE
CAN SURVIVE

MOVE SAFELY
THROUGH THIS
MAZE OF A LIFE
THAT WILL
SURROUND YOU SOMETIMES

LIVE WITH A THIRST.

33

SOMETIMES TOO MUCH ADVICE

by Barbara Brandon

about THE CONTRIBUTORS

LYNDA BARRY is a writer, painter, and cartoonist who was born in 1956 and now hangs out in the attic of a very old house in Evanston, Illinois. She was kind of a weird girl who grew up on a rundown street in Seattle, Washington, with a mother who was always screaming at her and many mean vampire girls for neighbors, so she spent most of her time alone reading, cutting pictures out of magazines, copying pictures off of album covers, and putting interesting clothes on her dog. The best decision she ever made was to go to college, where she finally met other weird people who did very interesting things, and they influenced her and pretty soon she was doing very interesting things all of the time until it became her actual JOB! What a *great job!* Barry has written nine books and a play and has had a lot of shows of her paintings. Her comic strip is in fifty newspapers, and she still loves to read and draw and cut pictures out of magazines, and every Halloween she dresses up like a horrible witch and dresses her dog up as a horrible tiger and together they run around the town looking for mean people to sneak up behind and scare. It has turned out to be a very good life for Lynda Barry! The title of her comix is "Mean Girls Are Real."

MARY CATHERINE BATESON teaches anthropology and English at George Mason University in Fairfax, Virginia. Her books include *Peripheral Visions,* which is about learning from other cultures; *Composing a Life,* a warm study of five women (including herself) who have lived creatively through complex lives; and *With a Daughter's Eye,* a memoir of her parents, anthropologists Gregory Bateson and Margaret Mead. The title of the essay she wrote for this book is "Being Alone/Being On Your Own."

BARBARA BRANDON of Brooklyn, New York, created the all-woman comic strip "Where I'm Coming From" in the early 1980s, but it wasn't until 1989 that these nine girlfriends got some play in the *Detroit Free Press.* In 1990, Universal Press Syndicate picked up the strip, and Sonya, Lekesia, Alisha, Cheryl, Nicole, Lydia and the rest of the gang eventually were talking their heads off in more than fifty newspapers around the nation. The crew can also be viewed in the privacy of their own book entitled—what else?—*Where I'm Coming From.* As for little Brianna, she's making her debut here, in the comic strip Brandon titled "Advice Is Nice."

JOAN JACOBS BRUMBERG is a historian and professor at Cornell University in Ithaca, New York. She writes and teaches about the history of adolescent girls, their bodies, and their diseases. Brumberg is the author of *Fasting Girls,* which describes how

148

anorexia nervosa was named and identified in the 1870s and why it has become so prevalent today, and *The Body Project: An Intimate History of American Girls.* The essay she wrote for this book is entitled "Talking to Yourself and to History."

SANDRA CISNEROS wrote "Eleven," the piece presented here, many, many years ago. "I wrote this story," she says, "because a children's press asked me to at a time when I was very poor and needed money. I wrote it, sent it, and it was immediately rejected as not being appropriate for children. But there is poetic justice. Since then it's been one of my most popular stories, especially loved and understood by kids. Maybe the children's press didn't want to publish sad stories, but painful memories like this one are the ones I remember the most. Perhaps writing is a way of remembering and forgetting all at once." Was Cisneros the little girl in "Eleven"? Well, kind of. "The core of the story is true," she says, "but it was *not* my birthday. The teacher was a nun, the sweater was not red—it was pink or white—and I did not have to put it on. I was eight years old." "Eleven" has been collected in Cisneros's book *Woman Hollering Creek and Other Stories,* featuring girls, women, and men living and learning life in Mexico and Texas. Another of her well-known books is *The House on Mango Street,* a series of scenes from the life of a girl named Esperanza (Hope, in English), growing up in the Latino section of Chicago, where Cisneros was born and raised.

JUDITH ORTIZ COFER, a native of Puerto Rico who spent much of her childhood in Paterson, New Jersey, began writing stories when she was quite young, inspired by all the reading she did in Spanish and English (with a particular fondness for fairy tales and folk tales). It was when she was in high school that she began writing poems. The one she wrote for this book is entitled "Notes to Tanya: Remember," and it was written for a very special person in her life: Tanya is her daughter. With this poem Cofer wanted to remind Tanya (and all of us) that "the world is not just a tiny room in which to do one thing—even if it is a good thing. It's a big world full of wonder and beauty." Cofer is the author of the novel *The Line of the Sun* (Spanish translation: *La linea del sol*); the collection of short stories *An Island Like You: Stories of the Barrio*; two books of poetry, *Terms of Survival* and *Reaching for the Mainland*; and three collections of prose and poetry, *Silent Dancing* (Spanish translation: *Bailando en silencio*), *The Latin Deli*, and *The Year of Our Revolution.* Her awards and honors include fellowships from the NEA and the Witter Bynner Foundation for poetry; selection of her work for the Sydicated Fiction Project; a PEN/Martha Albrand Special Citation in nonfiction for *Silent Dancing*; the Anisfield Wolf Book Award for *The Latin Deli*; and, for *An Island Like You*, a Best Book of the Year, 1995–96 by the American Library Association and the first Pura Belpre medal by REFORMA of ALA. HBO has optioned one of the stories in *The Latin Deli* for a feature-length movie. Cofer lives in Atlanta, Georgia, where she is a professor of English and creative writing at the University of Georgia.

JOHNNETTA B. COLE served as president of Spelman College from 1987 to 1997. She is on sabbatical during the academic year 1997–98. In the fall of 1998 she will begin her post at Emory University as Presidential Distinguished Professor of Anthropology, Women's Studies and African American Studies. Cole is the author of *Conversations: Straight Talk with America's Sister President* and *Dream the Boldest Dreams: And Other Lessons of Life,* and she is the editor of three textbooks: *Anthropology for the Eighties, Anthropology for the Nineties,* and *All American Women: Lines That Divide, Ties That Bind.* She lives in Atlanta, Georgia, with her husband and is the mother of three sons and two stepsons, as well as the surrogate mom of many young women.

SHARON CREECH is the author of *Walk Two Moons,* winner of the 1995 Newbery Medal, as well as *Pleasing the Ghost, Chasing Redbird,* and *Absolutely Normal Chaos,* from which her contribution to this book was taken. She spent most of her childhood in Cleveland, Ohio, where she grew up with a family almost identical to that of Mary Lou Finney's. She and her husband divide their time between England and Lake Chautauqua in western New York.

ANN DECKER, a veteran graphic designer currently working at *Fortune* magazine, is the founder and co-editor of the comic book *GirlTalk.* Her handiwork can also be seen in the anthologies *World War 3 Illustrated: Confrontational Comics* and *Mind Riot: Coming of Age in Comics,* as well as in her comic strip "Hairstories." She lives in Brooklyn, New York. "Be Careful What You Wish" is the title of the comix she created for this book.

REBECCA GOLDSTEIN was Samantha in the short story she wrote for this book, and which she's entitled "Strange." As she explains: "When I was a teenager, I spent quite a long time trying to figure out how other people thought, terrified of being different—of being strange—and I spent a good bit of energy trying to reshape my mind so that it would fit with everyone else's. I only wish someone had told me back then that different doesn't necessarily mean wrong. In fact, sometimes it means right, or at least interesting, or . . . well, just different." Goldstein's novels include *The Mind-Body Problem, The Dark Sister,* and *Mazel.* Her collection of short stories is entitled *Strange Attractors.* Among her many awards is the "Genius Award": a John D. and Catherine T. MacArthur Fellowship, a five-year grant for outstanding achievement in writing, which she received in 1996. She lives in Highland Park, New Jersey, with her husband and two daughters.

NICOLE HAISLETT, who grew up in St. Petersburg, Florida, was given her first dip in the pool when she was two months old. At age five she was on a local swim team. At age thirteen she was competing in the junior nationals. She went on to become an American and NCAA record holder in the 200-yard and 200-meter freestyle events, a thirteen-

time U.S. National Champion, a five-time U.S. Open Champion, and an eight-time NCAA Champion. At the 1990 Goodwill Games she won the 100-meter freestyle. At the World Championships in 1991 she took the gold in the 100-meter freestyle, the 400-meter freestyle relay, and the 400-meter medley relay. The three gold medals she won at the 1992 Summer Olympics in Barcelona, Spain (the most won by a U.S. athlete at those Games) were for the 200-meter freestyle, the 400-meter medley relay, and the 400-meter freestyle relay, in which her team set a world record. At the 1994 NCAAs, swimming for the University of Florida, Haislett won three events, including the 200-yard freestyle, which made her only the third woman ever to win the same event four times at the NCAAs. When she retired from competitive swimming, Haislett became the assistant women's coach at the University of Florida in Gainesville, where she earned her bachelor's degree in telecommunications, specializing in production.

ALICE HOFFMAN is the author of twelve novels: *Property Of*, *The Drowning Season*, *Angel Landing*, *White Horses*, *Fortune's Daughter*, *Illumination Night*, *At Risk*, *Seventh Heaven*, *Turtle Moon*, *Second Nature*, *Practical Magic*, and *Here on Earth*. Her first children's book is *Fireflies*. She lives near Boston.

LATOYA HUNTER shared episodes from her teenage life in *The Diary of Latoya Hunter: My First Year in Junior High School*. In this collection of conversations with "Janice," as she named her diary, Hunter reaffirmed, among other things, her desire to be a writer, in particular, a journalist. In 1995 she entered Concordia College in Bronxville, New York, declaring herself an English major early on. Hunter, who was born in Jamaica, West Indies, grew up in the Bronx and Mount Vernon, New York.

LAUREN HUTTON was trying to come up with the money for her passage on a steamer bound for Tangier, in the North African nation of Morocco, in 1964 when she stumbled upon a showroom modeling job. After nine months of having everyone in the modeling industry telling her to leave town (too short, too round, too gapped!), she was making modeling history. In 1974 she thought up the first exclusive talent contract in modeling history, with Revlon. It was a deal that changed modeling fees from hundreds to thousands and created the first of the "supermodels." Hutton has appeared on a record twenty-five *Vogue* magazine covers, and in editorial campaigns for a host of companies, including J. Crew, Giorgio Armani, and Barneys department store. Her many acting credits include roles in the films *American Gigolo*, with Richard Gere; *Once Bitten*, with Jim Carrey; and the recently completed children's story for Warner Brothers, *Monty Madrat*. Hutton started her own production company, Lula Films, with Luca Babini, in 1995. The five-night national talk show *Lauren Hutton and . . .* was one of the company's first endeavors. Another is the recently released docudrama *Little Warriors*, the story of her two godsons, who, prior to the younger boy's brain surgery, traveled to meet and live with their Masai counterparts on the Kenya-Tanzania border in East Africa. Hutton's current love is double-tank nitrox wreck-diving all over the world.

ELIZABETH JENKINS-SAHLIN was born in Stockholm, Sweden. Around the age of three she moved to the United States. After living in Greenwich, Connecticut, for a few years, her family moved to Old Greenwich, where she attended Eastern Middle School. Her favorite activities are writing, drawing, biking, in-line skating and in-line hockey, and ice-skating. She is also very musical. She plays the cello in the school orchestra, and loves to experiment and play around on other instruments as well. "Something to Celebrate" is the title of the mini family memoir she wrote for this book.

MAVIS JUKES is the author of several books for children and teenagers, including *Like Jake and Me, No One Is Going to Nashville, Blackberries in the Dark, Getting Even, Wild Iris Bloom, I'll See You in My Dreams, Expecting the Unexpected*, and *It's a Girl Thing: How to Stay Healthy, Safe, and in Charge*. Jukes, who is also an elementary school teacher, has volunteered as a lawyer in the area of juvenile defense. She lives in Northern California with her husband and two daughters.

M. E. KERR is the author of roughly twenty books for children and young adults, among them *I'll Love You When You're More Like Me; Is That You, Miss Blue?; Gentlehands; Dinky Hocker Shoots Smack!; Me Me Me Me Me: Not a Novel; Night Kites; Linger; Deliver Us from Evie; Hello, I Lied;* the Fell series; *And I Stay Near You*, and *Blood on the Forehead*. Her story included here, "We Might as Well All Be Strangers," was drawn from two real-life events. The 1993 American Library Association's Margaret A. Edwards Award for lifetime achievement is among her awards and honors. Kerr lives in East Hampton, New York.

JOYCE A. LADNER, a nationally known sociologist, has lectured and published extensively in the areas of teen pregnancy, diversity, higher education, urban issues, public policy, human sexuality, and child welfare. She is the author of a pioneering sociological study of black girls growing up in a housing project in St. Louis, *Tomorrow's Tomorrow*, and *Mixed Families: Adopting Across Racial Boundaries*; co-author of *Lives of Promise, Lives of Pain: Young Mothers After New Chance* (with Janet Quint and Judith Musick); editor of the anthology *The Death of White Sociology*; and co-editor of *Adolescence and Poverty: Challenge for the '90s* (with Peter Edelman). Ladner, a professor in the School of Social Work at Howard University for more than 16 years, made history when she became the first woman to serve as president of this university (1994–95). Her "extra-curricular" activities include a 1995 appointment by President

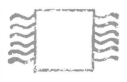

Clinton to the new District of Columbia Financial Control Board and membership on the Advisory Council on Violence Against Women. Her honors include a Wise Woman Award from the Center for Women's Policy Studies, a DuBois–Johnson Frazier Award for Outstanding Scholarship from the American Sociological Association, a Lee Founders Award from the Society for the Study of Social Problems, and a Joseph S. Himes Distinguished Career Award from the Association of Black Sociologists. Ladner is the mother of one son, Thomas, and mentor to many girls and young women. The title of the letter she wrote for this book is "Dear Sonia."

REBECCA LOBO, who was raised in Southwick, Massachusetts, played center/forward for the University of Connecticut's Huskies from 1991 to 1995. She was the first Big East basketball player in history to earn both the Big East Player of the Year and Scholar-Athlete of the Year awards (in 1994 and 1995). By 1995 she had become the most honored women's basketball player in the nation for her scholar-athlete achievements since Hall-of-Famer Anne Donovan. Her other awards and honors include Associated Press Female Athlete of the Year, Women's Sports Foundation Woman of the Year (Team Sports), the National Collegiate Athletic Association Woman of the Year, and two ESPYs—Female Athlete of the Year and Female College Basketball Player of the Year—all in 1995. Lobo was awarded a gold medal at the 1996 Summer Olympics as a member of the U.S. Olympic Basketball Team. In the fall of that year she signed with the Women's National Basketball Association and was assigned as a premier player to the WNBA's New York Liberty in January 1997. Lobo teamed up with her mother, RuthAnn Lobo, for a book about her basketball career and her mother's successful battle with breast cancer. The book is entitled *The Home Team*. The piece Rebecca Lobo wrote for this book is entitled "Ten Tenets."

NATALIE MERCHANT began her career as a singer and songwriter at the age of seventeen when she joined a folk-rock group in Jamestown, New York, called 10,000 Maniacs. She was the principal songwriter and lead singer of the group for twelve years. During this time the group's releases included the albums *Hope Chest*, *The Wishing Chair*, *In My Tribe*, *Blind Man's Zoo*, *Our Time in Eden*, and *10,000 Maniacs MTV Unplugged*. In 1993, Merchant left the group to begin a solo career, with the album *Tigerlily*. She has established herself as one of the most popular songwriters and singers in America today. She has been awarded three gold and six platinum records by the recording industry and has toured extensively throughout the United States and Europe. The name of the poem she wrote for this book is "Make a Cradle of Your Arms."

KYOKO MORI is the author of the memoir *The Dream of Water* and a book of essays, *Polite Lies*, as well as two novels for young adults: *Shizuko's Daughter*, the story of twelve-year-old Yuki, whose artwork is her salvation from a whirlwind of family problems;

and *One Bird,* the story of fifteen-year-old Megumi, who is enduring a difficult growing-up. She titled the essay she wrote for this book "Remembering a Girl Who Never Wanted to Become 'A Woman.'" Mori teaches creative writing at St. Norbert College in De Pere, Wisconsin, where she is often sighted not only running but also bird-watching and weaving.

JEANNE MOUTOUSSAMY-ASHE was born and raised in Chicago, Illinois, where her artistic education began at age eight, when her parents enrolled her in classes at the Art Institute of Chicago. Her work has been exhibited in numerous one-woman shows in the United States and abroad. Her books include *Daufuskie Island,* a photo essay about the Gullah-speaking people of a South Carolina sea island; *Viewfinders,* which documents the work of African American women photographers from as early as 1860; and *Daddy and Me,* a photographic essay of her husband, U.S. tennis champion Arthur Ashe, and their daughter, Camera. Moutoussamy-Ashe teaches photography at the Dalton School in New York City. The title of the piece she created for this book is "A Love of Self."

BERNICE JOHNSON REAGON, Distinguished Professor of History at American University and Curator Emeritus at the Smithsonian Institution, is a composer and singer performing with Sweet Honey In The Rock, the ensemble she founded in 1973. Her recent works include *We Who Believe in Freedom: Sweet Honey In The Rock Still on the Journey; We'll Understand It Better By and By: Pioneering African American Gospel Composers;* and the re-mastered *Voices of the Civil Rights Movement, 1960–1965,* a two-CD collection with booklet anthology. Bernice Johnson Reagon was conceptual producer and narrator of the Peabody award–winning twenty-six-hour radio series *Wade in the Water: African American Sacred Music Traditions,* produced by the Smithsonian Institution and National Public Radio, and curator for a traveling exhibition of the same title. She received the 1995 Charles Frankel Prize, a Presidential medal in recognition of her outstanding contribution to public understanding of the humanities. She lives in Washington, D.C. **TOSHI REAGON** is a musician, recording producer, composer, and band leader. She has been recording since she was fifteen and has several releases to her credit, among them "Rejected Stone" and "Kindness," her first acoustical recording. She has worked collaboratively with her mother in several projects, including as producer of Sweet Honey In The Rock recordings and live concert performances. She lives in Brooklyn, New York. Mother and daughter titled the piece they composed for this book "Everyday Revolutions; Or, Girl Stories Across Two Generations."

FAITH RINGGOLD is an internationally renowned artist, best known for her painted story quilts, soft sculptures, and masks. Her books for children of all ages include *Tar Beach, Aunt Harriet's Underground Railroad in the Sky, Dinner at Aunt Connie's House,*

My Dream of Martin Luther King, and *Bonjour, Lonnie.* You can chat with the author/artist in *Talking to Faith Ringgold* (co-authored with Linda Freeman and Nancy Roucher), and there's a larger "self-portrait" in *We Flew over the Bridge: The Memoirs of Faith Ringgold,* her first book for adults. *Dancing at the Louvre: Faith Ringgold's French Collection and Other Story Quilts* is the companion book to her solo exhibition curated by the New Museum of Contemporary Art in New York City, which began a six-city tour in January 1998. Ringgold is the mother of two daughters, Barbara and Michelle, and grandmother of three girls—Martha, Teddy, and Faith. The title of the fairy tale she created for this book is "The Five Queens."

ANITA RODDICK opened her first shop in 1976, in Brighton, England, about a forty-minute journey from where she grew up. She started this shop (with not a lot of money, by the way) because she wanted to earn a purposeful living: She wanted to make money at the same time that she served a need—in this case, for reasonably priced personal-care products that would be safe for consumers and the environment. Roddick has told of her adventures in life and business in the book *Body and Soul: Profits with Principles—The Amazing Success Story of Anita Roddick and The Body Shop.* The Body Shop is headquartered in Roddick's hometown of Littlehampton, where she lives with her husband, who also works at The Body Shop. "Travel Is Like a University Without Walls" is the title of the essay she wrote for this book.

GRETCHEN ROSENKRANZ lives in Olympia, Washington, with her parents and older sister, Shelley. She hopes for careers in writing and acting. After mastering swimming and wheelchair racing, she went on to tackle waterskiing, downhill snow skiing, and riding hand-cranked bikes. Hanging out with friends at the mall and going to dances and school-related sports activities are among her favorite things to do. Her hobbies include collecting teddy bears and spoons. "Imagine, Believe, and Make It Happen" is what she titled the essay she wrote for this book.

TABITHA SOREN is currently overcompensating for not being popular enough in junior high with a career in television. Soren is the MTV News senior political correspondent, winning the Peabody Journalism Award for her coverage of the 1992 Presidential campaign. She is also a freelance writer for the likes of *Elle* magazine, *USA Weekend,* and the New York Times Syndicate.

ISABEL CARTER STEWART is the national executive director of Girls Incorporated. Prior to joining this organization she served as director of program administration at the National Academy Foundation, a business and education partnership whose mission is to prepare young adults for school-to-work transitions. Earlier on in life, she was a teacher. Stewart, who lives in New York City, has two sons and, adding up all the girls who participate in Girls Incorporated affiliates, about a quarter-million daughters. "But Momma . . ." is the title of the essay she wrote for this book.

DEBORAH TANNEN, who was born in Brooklyn, New York, is a sociolinguist who has stepped across at least two divides: She moves back and forth between academia and the world at large, and between nonfiction and creative writing. She is University Professor and professor of linguistics at Georgetown University in Washington, D.C., where she has been on the faculty since receiving her Ph.D. in linguistics at the University of California, Berkeley, in 1979. Tannen is best known for her book *You Just Don't Understand: Women and Men in Conversation,* which was on the *New York Times* best seller list for nearly four years and has been translated into twenty-four languages. Her most recent book is *Talking from 9 to 5: Women and Men in the Workplace: Language, Sex, and Power.* In addition to her fourteen books on language, she has published a book about the work of a modern Greek novelist (Lilika Nakos) and essays, short stories, and poems. Her play about her father, *An Act of Devotion,* is included in *Best Short Plays 1994–1995* and was produced along with her play *Sisters* by Horizons Theatre in Arlington, Virginia, in spring 1995. She is pleased that her essay "Daddy Young and Old," also about her father, is included in the book *Family: American Writers Remember Their Own.* The title of the essay she wrote for this book is "Why Boys Don't Know What Girls Mean and Girls Think Boys Are Mean." This is the first time Tannen has written for a young audience, and she is "glad the time has come."

VERA WANG began to make heads turn in the fashion world in 1990 when she opened the Vera Wang Bridal House in New York City (a shop in which a bride-to-be could be completely outfitted from head to toe) and Vera Wang Made-to-Order, with one-of-a-kind wedding-day sensations and evening dresses. In 1992 she launched the Vera Wang Bridal Collection, a line of wedding dresses sold only at exclusive stores. In 1993 came Vera Wang's Ready-to-Wear Collection, devoted to evening wear, and in 1995 VWBC by Vera Wang, an extensive collection of bridesmaid dresses, and Vera Wang footwear. Her piece for this book is an adaptation of "Designing Woman," which originally appeared in the 1995 Chapin School Alumnae Bulletin.

WENDY WASSERSTEIN, a graduate of the Yale School of Drama, is the author of a number of hit Broadway plays, including *The Heidi Chronicles,* winner of the 1989 Pulitzer Prize in drama and Tony Award for best play, and *The Sisters Rosensweig,* recipient of the 1993 Outer Critics Award. Other plays include *Uncommon Women and Others, Isn't It Romantic,* and *An American Daughter.* The essay included in this book, "Pappagallo Jungle," is taken from her book *Bachelor Girls.*

SIGOURNEY WEAVER started her career in the New York theater. She made her film debut as Officer Ripley in *Alien* (1979) and has repeated the role in three sequels: *Aliens* (1986), *Alien 3* (1992), and *Alien Resurrection* (1997). Some of the other films she has starred in are *Ghostbusters*, *The Year of Living Dangerously*, *Gorillas in the Mist*, *Working Girl*, and *Death in the Maiden*. Sigourney Weaver continues to act in the theater and her production company, Goat Cay Productions, is dedicated to introducing new talents from the world of theater into the world of film. Her piece for this book is an adaptation of a commencement address she delivered in June 1990 at The Chapin School.

JULIANN F. WILLEY earned degrees in genetic engineering, biology, and chemistry at Cedar Crest College in Allentown, Pennsylvania. After college she did research in molecular biology and then went on to her first job as a forensic chemist with the Office of the Chief Medical Examiner for the State of Delaware. In 1991 she became a forensic microscopist with the newly built Delaware State Police Crime Lab and two years later became its first civilian and first female director. Willey came into the slogan "Chemistry class led me to a life of crime" as a result of participating in the campaign titled Expect the Best from a Girl. That's What You'll Get, which was launched in 1995 by the Advertising Council and the Women's College Coalition. She says she never realized science would give her the opportunity of a lifetime to be featured in television, radio, and print ads nationwide. Her involvement with this campaign has also given her the opportunity to address audiences of all ages with her message about women and careers in the sciences. Willey, who grew up in Wilmington, Delaware, lives in Middletown, Delaware, with her husband and their two sons. Her title for the detective work she did for this book is "An 'Analysis Report' on Girls and Science."

about the editor

TONYA BOLDEN is the author of the children's book *Through Loona's Door: A Tammy and Owen Adventure with Carter G. Woodson*. Her books for teenagers include the novels *Mama, I Want to Sing* (co-authored with Vy Higginsen) and *Just Family*; the anthology *Rites of Passage: Stories About Growing Up by Black Writers from Around the World*; and a collection of biographies of ten epic women, *And Not Afraid to Dare*. Her books for grownups include *The Book of African-American Women: 150 Crusaders, Creators, and Uplifters*.

ACKNOWLEDGMENTS

We gratefully acknowledge the following for permission to use their work in this book.

LYNDA BARRY for "Mean Girls Are Real." Copyright © 1998 by Lynda Barry. Used by permission of the artist.

MARY CATHERINE BATESON for "Being Alone/Being on Your Own." Copyright © 1998 by Mary Catherine Bateson. Used by permission of the author.

BARBARA BRANDON for "Advice Is Nice," a special edition of "Where I'm Coming From," distributed by Universal Press Syndicate. Copyright © 1998 by Barbara Brandon. Used by permission of the artist.

JOAN JACOBS BRUMBERG for "Talking to Yourself and to History." Copyright © 1998 by Joan Jacobs Brumberg. Used by permission of the author.

SANDRA CISNEROS for "Eleven," from *Woman Hollering Creek.* Copyright © 1991 by Sandra Cisneros. Published by Vintage Books, a division of Random House, Inc., New York, and originally published in hardcover by Random House, Inc. Used by permission of Susan Bergholz Literary Services.

JUDITH ORTIZ COFER for "Notes to Tanya: Remember." Copyright © 1998 by Judith Ortiz Cofer. Used by permission of the author.

JOHNNETTA B. COLE for "Follow Your Passion." Copyright © 1998 by Johnnetta B. Cole. Used by permission of the author.

SHARON CREECH for excerpts from *Absolutely Normal Chaos.* Copyright © 1990 by Sharon Creech. First published in Great Britain in 1990 by Macmillan Children's Books, used by permission of HarperCollins Publishers.

ANN DECKER for "Be Careful What You Wish." Copyright © 1998 by Ann Decker. Used by permission of the artist.

REBECCA GOLDSTEIN for "Strange." Copyright © 1998 by Rebecca Goldstein. Used by permission of the author.

NICOLE HAISLETT for "It Takes More Than Talent to Be a Winner." Copyright © 1998 by Nicole Haislett. Used by permission of the author.

ALICE HOFFMAN for "Nothing Is as Healing as a Book." Copyright © 1998 by Alice Hoffman. Used by permission of the author.

LATOYA HUNTER for "Dear Diary." Copyright © 1998 by Latoya Hunter. Used by permission of the author. The Maya Angelou excerpt from *And Still I Rise* Copyright © 1978 by Maya Angelou. Reprinted by permission of Random House, Inc.

LAUREN HUTTON for "Interview with Tonya Bolden." Copyright © 1998 by Lauren Hutton. Used by permission of Lauren Hutton.

ELIZABETH JENKINS-SAHLIN for "Something to Celebrate." Copyright © 1998 by Elizabeth Jenkins-Sahlin. Used by permission of the author.

MAVIS JUKES for "Help Is Out There" Copyright © 1998 by Mavis Jukes. Used by permission of the author.

M. E. KERR for "We Might As Well All Be Strangers" by M. E. Kerr, from *Am I Blue: Coming Out from the Silence,* edited by Marion Dane Bauer. Text copyright © 1994 by M. E. Kerr, text copyright © 1994 by Marion Dane Bauer. Used by permission of HarperCollins Publishers.

JOYCE A. LADNER for "Dear Sonia." Copyright © 1998 by Joyce Ladner. Used by permission of the author.

REBECCA LOBO for "Ten Tenets." Copyright © 1998 by Rebecca Lobo. Used by permission of the author.

NATALIE MERCHANT for "Make a Cradle of Your Arms." Copyright © 1998 by Natalie Merchant. Used by permission of the author.

KYOKO MORI for "Remembering a Girl Who Never Wanted to Become 'A Woman.'" Copyright © 1998 by Kyoko Mori. Used by permission of the author.

JEANNE MOUTOUSSAMY-ASHE for "A Love of Self." Copyright © 1998 by Jeanne Moutoussamy-Ashe. Used by permission of the photographer.

BERNICE JOHNSON REAGON & TOSHI REAGON for "Everyday Revolutions; Or, Girl Stories Across Two Generations." Copyright © 1998 by Bernice Johnson Reagon & Toshi Reagon. Used by permission of the authors.

FAITH RINGGOLD for "The Five Queens." Copyright © 1998 by Faith Ringgold. Used by permission of the author.

ANITA RODDICK for "Travel Is Like a University Without Walls." By Anita Roddick, © The Body Shop, UK, 1998. All rights reserved.

GRETCHEN ROSENKRANZ for "Imagine, Believe, and Make It Happen." Copyright © 1998 by Gretchen Rosenkranz. Used by permission of the author.

TABITHA SOREN for "Popularity Peaks." Copyright © 1998 by Tabitha Soren. Used by permission of the author.

ISABEL CARTER STEWART for "But, Momma . . ." Copyright © 1998 by Isabel Carter Stewart. Used by permission of the author. "Girls' Bill of Rights" © 1992 Girls Incorporated. Used by permission of Girls Incorporated.

DEBORAH TANNEN for "Why Boys Don't Know What Girls Mean and Girls Think Boys Are Mean." Copyright © 1998 by Deborah Tannen. Used by permission of the author.

VERA WANG for an adaptation of "Designing Woman" from the 1995 Chapin Alumnae Bulletin. Copyright © 1998 by Vera Wang. Used by permission of the author.

WENDY WASSERSTEIN for "Pappagallo Jungle" from *Bachelor Girls* by Wendy Wasserstein. Copyright © 1990 by Wendy Wasserstein. Reprinted by permission of Alfred A. Knopf, Inc.

SIGOURNEY WEAVER for an adaptation of the June 1990 Commencement address at The Chapin School in New York City as printed in the Chapin Alumnae Bulletin. Copyright © 1990 by Sigourney Weaver. Used by permission of the author.

JULIANN F. WILLEY for "An 'Analysis Report' on Girls and Science." Copyright © 1998 by Juliann F. Willey. Used by permission of the author.